THE SECRET BEHIND PAUL'S THORN IN THE FLESH

By Mel Berg

The Secret Behind Paul's Thorn In The Flesh
by Mel Berg

Printed in the United States of America

ISBN 9781615794799

Unless otherwise indicated, Bible quotations are taken from The King James Version of the Bible.

Mel Berg Ministries, Inc.
8922 Quigley
Westminster, Colorado 80031
303-429-2277
E-mail: itsahitsong@msn.com

www.xulonpress.com

1/7/10

Mary + Bill,

Discover more of Christ.

Mel Berg

“Howbeit when he, the Spirit of truth, is come, he will guide you into all truth: for he shall not speak of himself; but whatsoever he shall hear, that shall he speak: and he will shew you things to come.” (John 16:13

“But the anointing which ye have received of him abideth in you, and ye need not that any man teach you: but as the same anointing teacheth you of all things, and is truth, and is no lie, and even as it hath taught you, ye shall abide in him.” (1 John 2:27)

ABOUT THE AUTHOR

Mel formerly owned Alpha & Omega Distributors, a company that marketed Christian books and Bibles to supermarkets and Christian book stores for over fifteen years. He was employed by David C. Cook Company for another six years, managing rack jobbing inventory throughout the United States.

Mel has recorded ten country gospel albums. A few years ago, his recording, Oasis of Love, was number one on the God's Country international chart. For radio, he produced "Country Anointing," a Saturday night Christian program heard on KJNP in North Pole, Alaska. The program continued as a rerun for several years.

Songs he has written include: Quick Draw to Forgive, Life Is Like An Auction, How Far Would You Go, Did Not Our Hearts Burn, Have You Heard The Country Boy Sing, The Law, Heaven a Little More Real and many more.

He has produced a special Country Gospel Music cassette tape and CD for truck drivers for Truck Stop Chapel in Watkins, Colorado, and Truck Stop Chapel in Big Springs, Nebraska. Thousands of copies have been given away in ministry to truck drivers.

The last 14 years, Mel has been in full-time ministry, singing country gospel music at more than 400 nursing homes and retirement centers throughout the Western states, performing more than 300 concerts a year.

Mel and his wife Mary live in Westminster, Colorado, and have three children and six grandchildren.

ACKNOWLEDGEMENTS

I'm forever thankful for my Lord and Savior for revealing the secret behind Paul's thorn in the flesh to me and inspiring me to write this book. What a glorious revelation and source of truth for daily living. This knowledge has helped me write books and songs of the Gospel that I hope and pray will be fruitful to the Kingdom of heaven.

To my wife, Mary and our children and grandchildren that I love so dearly. I point you to Jesus Christ as the way, the truth and the life.

To my editors, Norma Mummert and Lois Waldschmidt for their super job.

To Todd Daniels for your encouragement and title suggestion.

To all my special friends that I've met over the years. If I named just some of you, there would not be room enough for all that I could list. You know who you are. You have touched my life.

To Berniece Farris, who is 87 years young, who first heard me sing, 'Life Is Like An Auction' at the Senior Center in Cheyenne, Wyoming. It touched her heart and took away the depression that had her bound from recent sorrows. Berniece lost her son in the Vietnam war on January 12, 1969 and so to help her through her great loss, she has volunteered countless hours of her time to the Veterans Administrations in Cheyenne over the last forty years. What a blessing to see her interaction and love for injured soldiers that fought for our nation's freedom and the freedom of other nations. She comes to many of my concerts and has made over 2000 pillows for those in nursing homes and retirement centers. You are something the Lord needs more of. Berniece, I dedicate this book to you, for helping me share the love of Christ through my songs.

FORWARD

Why me? Why should I write about Paul's thorn in the flesh? Ultimate understanding came to me while living the cross, in Christ, doing what the Word showed me and spending hours in prayer seeking truth from the Holy Spirit.

Before that time, I had read very little of the Bible and had never studied it. Consequently, as I faithfully began to read the Bible, Jesus Christ became the way, the truth and the life to me. One day I was amazed to find Scripture I already knew in my spirit, but had never read before.

> "That in the dispensation of the fullness of times he might gather together in one all things **in Christ**, both which are in heaven, and which are on earth; even in him:" (Eph. 1:10)

The reason I knew some Scripture before I read it was because I was following the dictates of the Holy Spirit. I applied the Word in real time at my work place. I dreamed it. I ate it. I took it with me everywhere I went. I put on the robe of righteousness. I was in Christ, and Christ was in me. I was addicted to the ministry of the saints of old. I wanted to learn more of what they knew as I faithfully served the Lord.

The Scripture account of Paul's thorn in the flesh really grabbed my attention. It captivated me! It dominated my thinking. You see, God had revealed to me what it was just days before I read it in the Bible. When I saw it—I was amazed; I had not heard about it or read about it before. I knew its secret. I felt honored. I trembled! Its truth was intriguing. It was complex and brilliant!

Later, I found it was a hidden mystery to scholars. It has made wise men search in vain. At my first understanding, I had a few missing pieces, too. It was as though the Lord required consecrated communion with Him to uncover the rest of the puzzle. It was worth the commitment to me. My heart longed to know the deeper things of God. I prayed to know more of God. I searched the Scriptures and found five major components of the thorn in the flesh.

It took fourteen years of prayer and Bible reading to find one of the missing pieces. It was profound. It takes all the pieces of a puzzle to see the beauty of a picture. To explain the mystery, after more than forty years of Bible study, I will need the Lord's help to paint, with words, the picture of the thorn in the flesh. As a picture is like a thousand words, perhaps one perfect word will paint a thousand pictures. Ultimately, I hope the picture you will see is the call of God to the cross with **Jesus Christ alive in you**.

PURPOSE OF THIS BOOK

- To reveal the true identity of the thorn in the flesh. With this knowledge, the seeker of God can understand, evaluate, compare and teach Scripture that has been hidden from the Body of Christ.
- To reaffirm the believer in the Holy Bible and his walk with God in truth.
- To reveal the impact the mystery had for the ministry of the Gospel.
- To lay out the timeline as to when the thorn developed in the Apostle Paul.
- To bring closure to false teachings that mislead students of the Holy Bible.
- To show the wisdom and creativity of our heavenly Father as manifested in the message of the Gospel.
- To reveal the five components of one of the greatest mysteries in the Bible.
- To show how the thorn in the flesh manifested itself in my life.

The truth of the thorn in the flesh is available to all who abide in Jesus Christ and live to honor and glorify His Holy Name. It will remain a secret and hidden until you, as a believer, search it out and the search begins at the cross. It is for all who will search the Scriptures to live **in Christ** and have a daily walk with the Lord. This book will delight you with the Gospel as you learn about this great spiritual mystery. The journey will provide deep insights and give you a new perspective for spiritual living.

PREFACE

There are many views as to what Paul's thorn in the flesh was:

1) Myth #1: **People**.
2) Myth #2: **Poor eyesight**.
3) Myth #3: A **messenger from Satan who** came to buffet Paul.
4) Myth #4: The **unknown**.
5) Myth #5: A physical **infirmity**.
6) Myth #6: **Physical limitations**.

Most commentators show that the purpose of the thorn was to keep Paul humble. However, in my study of the Scriptures I have found there is much more to the thorn than just the development of humility in Paul. When we look at the wisdom of God in other examples in the Bible, we'll see it clearly.

"The secret things belong unto the LORD our God: but those things which are revealed belong unto us and to our children for ever, that we may do all the words of this law." (Deut. 29:29)

Every word in the Bible has great significance in meaning and purpose. Isn't it God's will that we, as believers, know His Word?

It has been my experience to make wonderful discoveries about our Lord as I pray, study the Word and write. Therefore, I'm praying that the author of the Word of God, the Holy Spirit, be my spiritual editor as I write for the glory and honor of Jesus Christ.

"Knowing this first, that no prophecy of the Scripture is of any private interpretation. For the prophecy came not in old time by the will of man: but holy men of God spake as they were moved by the Holy Ghost." (2 Peter 1:20-21)

This book is for anyone who has a deep love for the Word of God, an intense interest in Bible study and the unveiling of the age-old mystery of Paul's thorn in the flesh.

"Behold, I waited for your words; I gave ear to your reasons, whilst ye searched out what to say." (Job 32:11)

THE THORN IN THE FLESH

"It is not expedient for me doubtless to glory. I will come to visions and revelations of the Lord. I knew a man in Christ above fourteen years ago, (whether in the body, I cannot tell; or whether out of the body, I cannot tell: God knoweth;) such an one caught up to the third heaven. And I knew such a man, (whether in the body, or out of the body, I cannot tell: God knoweth;) How that he was caught up into paradise, and heard unspeakable words, which it is not lawful for a man to utter.

"Of such an one will I glory: yet of myself I will not glory, but in mine infirmities. For though I would desire to glory, I shall not be a fool; for I will say the truth: but now I forbear, lest any man should think of me above that which he seeth me to be, or that he heareth of me.

"And lest I should be exalted above revelations, there was given to me **a thorn in the flesh,** the messenger of Satan to buffet me, lest I should be exalted above measure." (2 Cor. 12:1-7)

The experience that Paul wrote about in this passage was truly a supernatural event. God did something for Paul that was heavenly. To identify with it, we must start by asking the Holy Spirit to open our spiritual eyes and ears to understand it through a biblical and spiritual process. The only way this can be explained is through the guidance of the Holy Spirit. This may be the reason there are so many views: most are looking at it from a natural, physical point of view.

To validate the different views, the question must be asked: Would any of these beliefs demonstrate conviction (as truth) in a righteous court of law? What if they were cross-examined with the Holy Bible by holy men, who are born again, abiding in Christ, walking in the Word of God, living a sanctified Holy life in obedience to the law of the Spirit of life in Jesus Christ and serving to please God by a daily personal biblical cross-examination of their own person?

A Bible topic or subject view is only viable when it is supported by Scripture. The thought process must match verses with other verses in truth to the Gospel. Truth always agrees. Truth is conviction.

In the Holy Bible, the Son always agrees with the Father and Holy Spirit as one. If you read the Holy Bible and don't agree with God, you've just wasted your time. This is why many do not come to a saving knowledge of Jesus Christ:

they refuse to accept Jesus as the way to God. Some seek to intellectualize every word or passage in the Bible—the truth is hidden from many who take this approach.

> "For there are three that bear record in heaven, the Father, the Word, and the Holy Ghost: and these three are one. And there are three that bear witness in earth, the spirit, and the water, and the blood: and these three agree in one." (1 John 5:7-8)

I begin this subject knowing the author of the Word of God, having a sincere heart for the truth and devoting hours in prayer as I study the Holy Scriptures.

I ask the Holy Spirit to search my heart so that my words will have His abiding presence. I pray that He will direct the study of this subject to reveal truth, so that a clear choice can be made as to what Paul's thorn in the flesh was by:

1) Knowing that Jesus Christ and the cross are the foundation of truth;
2) Evaluating what past biblical scholars have written about Paul's thorn to see if each view agrees with the Holy Bible;
3) Interviewing today's pastors, biblical professors, teachers and scholars about each one's view of the thorn in the flesh;

4) Confirming Scriptures that point to the subject and its purpose to rightly divide the word of truth;
5) Showing that any interpretation of Scripture regarding the thorn in the flesh cannot be truth if the view doesn't point to Jesus Christ, the cross, or fit the Holy nature and **character of God;**
6) Demonstrating authority on the subject by logic, truth and fact from the Scripture, supported by the volume of logistical points of truth made to reveal the thorn in the flesh; and
7) Showing doctrine in every point of view.

"Shew me thy ways, O Lord; teach me thy paths. Lead me in thy truth, and teach me: for thou art the God of my salvation; on thee do I wait all the day." (Ps. 25:4-5)

"Teach me thy way, O Lord; I will walk in thy truth: unite my heart to fear thy name." (Ps. 86:11)

"I will worship toward thy holy temple, and praise thy name for thy lovingkindness and for thy truth: for thou hast magnified thy word above all thy name." (Ps. 138:2)

"Buy the truth, and sell it not; also wisdom, and instruction, and understanding." (Prov. 23:23)

HOW GOD FIRST REVEALED THE SECRET TO ME

About 5:00 one morning, as I was driving to work in Boulder, Colorado, I was in prayer and union with the Lord. I'd been studying and reading the Word for many weeks, doing everything the Word convicted my heart to do. I feared God. I was in tune to every word the preacher had spoken in all services I attended. My heart, mind and soul, at this very moment, were in obedience to the Word and following the dictates of the Holy Spirit. As I drove, I prayed for knowledge and wisdom.

Many will agree there are some things about God that cannot be known; God has to reveal them. One was acknowledged when the Lord revealed to me what Paul's thorn in the flesh was. This was the day God began to send data to my brain by supernatural high-speed that made me beg—"slow down." God was down-loading knowledge and wisdom to me. It was an intricate Divine code, very profound, holding deep meanings, bearing life's boundaries and heavenly properties. I pondered it intensely. Still, it was simple. I could have tried to explain it; but my limited skills of communication needed comprehensive study and time. Ultimately, I would need approval from the Lord.

> <u>"A wise man will hear, and will increase learning; and a man of understanding shall attain unto wise counsels: To understand a proverb, and the interpretation; the words of the wise, and their dark sayings. The fear of the LORD is the beginning of knowledge: but fools despise wisdom and instruction." (Prov. 1:5-7)</u>

Now, after more than forty years of walking in the Word, I humbly and reverently seek the Lord's permission and the Holy Spirit's guidance to give a convincing description of the thorn in the flesh that was revealed to me by the Lord on that day.

One of the first truths to address before I reveal the secret, is that it is very important that the enemy, the accuser of the brethren—Satan—be first disarmed by the power of the written Word of God and thereby made incompetent and helpless in his attempt to confuse the reader.

To do this, I present truth from the Word and testimonies found in the Holy Bible; using mostly the lives of Abraham, Isaac, Jacob, Moses, Jonah, David, Asaph, Jews, Gentiles, Ananias, Barnabas, Peter, James, John and Paul. Yet, the main players are Peter, James and John. These three men were the most intimate disciples of Jesus Christ and have key information for unraveling the mystery.

Therefore, to initiate the writing of this book, I begin by making the assertion that God showed me that Paul's thorn in the flesh was **his call** to be an apostle of Jesus Christ. It appears to be a paradox. **(Note: It is important to know what Paul prayed to have removed; it was never against the call, as we will see later in this book.)** Read on and you'll see it! The call pricked his natural flesh (first-born sin nature) to die daily and live in the cross, in the law of the Spirit of life in Jesus Christ. Paul followed the dictates of the Holy Spirit as he pressed toward the mark for the prize of the high calling of God in Jesus Christ.

Hereafter, let all who read and ponder the interpretation of the thorn in the flesh as the call, consider the appeal that it makes for a holy character to represent the Word of God. To understand the discovery, a walk must be done through passages of Scripture that make viable connections to the subject. As you read and ponder all the evidence that is brought forth, I humbly pray that the Holy Spirit will guide you in the Word. For no one can possibly understand the thorn in the flesh (the call) without knowing or being in Jesus Christ.

> "In him was life; and the life was the light of men. And the light shineth in darkness; and the darkness comprehended it not." (John 1:4-5)

He is the life and the light that brings us out of darkness. Do you remember when you first discovered the truth to something? His life brings us into truth that determines victory over defeat. I found the quickest way to find truth is to bow down at the cross, at the feet of Jesus Christ—fully surrendering, submitting to the Word of God and following the dictates of the Holy Spirit.

In the search for truth to spiritual questions it is absolutely essential to know the Scripture references of the character of God. His character is found throughout the pages of the Holy Bible.

> "But let him that glorieth glory in this, that he understandeth and knoweth me, that I am the Lord which exercise lovingkindness, judgment, and righteousness, in the earth: for in these things I delight, saith the Lord." (Jer 9:24)

1) Lovingkindness - God is love.
2) Judgment - There is a penalty for sin.
3) Righteousness - He is holy and made a way for sinners to escape the penalty of sin through Jesus Christ.

The cross is the place where God's ultimate character was displayed to a world of lost sinners.

Jesus Christ revealed God and His nature when He walked on earth with his disciples. The Word also reveals the character of God and guides us to know the will of God. Jesus is the only one that can reveal God to you. This is done by inviting Him into your heart. There is no other way to find God or to know God. Jesus is the answer to why we are here, who we are and where we will be with Him.

> "For there is one God, and one mediator between God and men, the man Christ Jesus;" (1 Tim. 2:5)

There is no short cut to explain the call as the thorn in the flesh; you must walk in the Word to know it. I challenge you to **do the walk.** In the ensuing Scriptures, you will find connecting links that show **the call** as Paul's thorn in the flesh. If you jump over Scripture and miss one of the important associations of Scripture, you will be unconnected to the union of spiritual progression and not be able to communicate or evaluate fully the thorn in the flesh—its beauty, its purpose and its powerful properties.

MYTH #1

PEOPLE (ASIAN JEWS AND JUDAIZERS TOO) AS THE THORN

Writers who identify Paul's thorn in the flesh as **people** believe that **Satan incited people** to come against Paul and the Gospel. One writer said Paul had a dedicated group of thorns as the thorn in the flesh.

The only Scripture that has any resemblance to people being thorns is found in the Book of Numbers, chapter 33. The reference is made about what would happen to the people of Israel if they didn't drive out the inhabitants of the land; the **people** left in the land would become, "pricks in your eyes and thorns in your sides."

> "But if ye will not drive out the inhabitants of the land from before you; then it shall come to pass, that

> those which ye let remain of them shall be pricks in your eyes, and thorns in your sides, and shall vex you in the land wherein ye dwell." (Num. 33:55)

The inhabitants of the land were an abomination to God because they worshiped foreign gods and idols. These **people** did not seek to know God intimately or have faith in God. They were fully occupied with delighting in sensual pleasures and material goods and were an irreligious or hedonistic people. They were a people clothed in fleshly desires.

Webster says that hedonism is the doctrine that pleasure or happiness is the sole or chief goal in life. Therefore, history has repeated itself because when we look around, we see that we live in a hedonistic society motivated by the pleasure principle.

> "For ye know how we have dwelt in the land of Egypt; and how we came through the nations which ye passed by; And ye have seen their abominations, and their idols, wood and stone, silver and gold, which were among them:) Lest there should be among you man, or woman, or family, or tribe, whose heart turneth away this day from the Lord our God, to go and serve the gods of these nations; lest there should be among you a root that beareth gall and wormwood;" (Deut. 29:16-18)

"And it come to pass, when he heareth the words of this curse, that he bless himself in his heart, saying, I shall have peace, though I walk in the imagination of mine heart, to add drunkenness to thirst: The Lord will not spare him, but then the anger of the Lord and his jealousy shall smoke against that man, and all the curses that are written in this book shall lie upon him, and the Lord shall blot out his name from under heaven." (Deut. 29:19-20)

GOD WANTED A PEOPLE TO BE CALLED AFTER HIS NAME

"Now the LORD had said unto Abram, Get thee out of thy country, and from thy kindred, and from thy father's house, unto a land that I will shew thee: And I will make of thee a great nation, and I will bless thee, and make thy name great; and thou shalt be a blessing: And I will bless them that bless thee, and curse him that curseth thee: and in thee shall all families of the earth be blessed." (Gen. 12:1-3)

Abraham obeyed the Lord and became our father of faith. Isaac, Abraham's son of promise, was the seed of promise to become a special people separated unto God. Abraham and his children were charged not to mix with other nations or races of people.

> "And I will establish my covenant between me and thee and thy seed after thee in their generations for an everlasting covenant, to be a God unto thee, and to thy seed after thee. And I will give unto thee, and to thy seed after thee, the land wherein thou art a stranger, all the land of Canaan, for an everlasting possession; and I will be their God. And God said unto Abraham, Thou shalt keep my covenant therefore, thou, and thy seed after thee in their generations." (Gen. 17:7-9)

If we view **people** as the thorn in the flesh, as in Numbers chapter 33, we have a problem: they were a people already judged by God as corrupt, and God didn't want His people to become like the **people** now living in the land. God charged His people to drive them out of the land. What is missing from the Numbers account is an example of humility. The thorn was to keep Paul from being exalted.

If there was a passage of Scripture in Numbers making reference to keeping the children of Israel from being exalted above measure, then perhaps it would be a point in case; but it doesn't match Scripture with the subject or the character of God.

Webster says humility is not proud or haughty; not arrogant or assertive. Reflecting, expressing, or offered in a spirit of deference or submission, is a humble apology. Its ranking is low in a hierarchy or scale.

Humility is considered one of the principal characteristics of the Lord Jesus Christ. Humility is like being not guilty of a crime, and yet accepting the penalty. No one can be humble without obedience—the cross revealed Jesus' humility.

Satan is the head of evil and directs the fallen angels as his messengers. He is the great adversary to God. The devil's character is prideful, and he works to exalt the flesh. Satan's access to mankind is through the sin nature. He is the stage-manager of the sin nature. He uses the carnal flesh to show evil through emotions, wicked thoughts and imaginings, forbidden sex, what is spoken or in deeds.

> "Now the works of the flesh are manifest, which are these; Adultery, fornication, uncleanness, lasciviousness, Idolatry, witchcraft, hatred, variance, emulations, wrath, strife, seditions, heresies, Envyings, murders, drunkenness, revellings, and such like: of the which I tell you before, as I have also told you in time past, that they which do such things shall not inherit the kingdom of God." (Gal. 5:19-21)

The Promised Land was inhabited by this kind of people. God foreknew that if these sinful **people** were left in the land, they would be a corruptible influence on God's people, causing sin. They would totally disrupt God's plan to build a holy nation, a royal priesthood, a people set apart, who would show the praises of Him who called them out of darkness into His marvelous light.

It does not make sense to think that **people** will keep you humble. How could that be possible? They were an enemy that God had judged as evil. God doesn't use evil to teach His children the way to live humbly. That is not the character of God.

If people were the thorn in the flesh, the nation of Israel would be the most humble people on earth. It has had **4,000** years of persecution. However, sin is the problem and not people. The cross is the only answer for that problem. This should clearly nix the idea that **people** were Paul's thorn in the flesh.

Nations have taken control of other nations and converted them to another ideology with success. But, when it comes to religion and the worship of idols or a false god, it is unlikely that you will change that nation. Ponder for a moment Sodom and Gomorrah. Are we any different? Who is producing most of the films and movies for our young people today? Is it not Sin Nature Studios or Sin Nature Productions?

> "Forasmuch then as Christ hath suffered for us in the flesh, arm yourselves likewise with the same mind: for he that hath suffered in the flesh hath ceased from sin; That he no longer should live the rest of his time in the flesh to the lusts of men, but to the will of God." (1 Peter 4:1-2)

God's Word is for the purpose of revealing God's character so that our behavior can be lived in example to His. He is looking for righteousness—not foreign gods or idols living in our house. What example do we see around us that would cause concern? I pray that you and I know the difference.

There have always been people in opposition to the truth, going their own way instead of living for the Lord. No one would question that Satan is busy corrupting lives. Satan is controlling people over vast areas of the earth. He is inciting people daily to rebel against God.

This teaching is saying that the thorn in the flesh was that Satan incited people to come against Paul, thus hindering the ministry of the Gospel. Yet the following Scripture shows the Jews coming against Paul, and not the inhabitants. His own people, the Jews, would be the thorn if that were the case. Therefore, this would rule out this view from being the thorn in the flesh.

> "But **the Jews stirred up** the devout and honourable women, and the chief men of the city, and raised persecution against Paul and Barnabas, and expelled them out of their coasts." (Acts 13:50)

Let us first put into context what the Scripture is saying just ahead of this comment about persecution, so we know the story line.

"Then Paul and Barnabas waxed bold, and said, It was necessary that the word of God should first have been spoken to you: but seeing ye put it from you, and judge yourselves unworthy of everlasting life, lo, we turn to the Gentiles.

"For so hath the Lord commanded us, saying, I have set thee to be a light of the Gentiles, that thou shouldest be for salvation unto the ends of the earth.

"And when the Gentiles heard this, they were glad, and glorified the word of the Lord: and as many as were ordained to eternal life believed. And the word of the Lord was published throughout all the region." (Acts 13:46-49)

Here we have the Gentiles being given the Word of God because the Jews were rejecting it. We see that if Satan thought he could gain ground by way of persecution, it backfired on him. It is because of persecution that the Word was published throughout the entire region. Even today, the persecuted church around the world is the most bold and where revival is the greatest.

When we first receive the Gospel, the joy of it excites us to sell out to God to take the Gospel to the world. We want everyone we meet to have it, too. It creates a giving spirit in our hearts.

The Gentiles received the truth eagerly; they understood more clearly what Jesus had done on the cross for them.

Through the messages of Paul and Barnabas, they realized this gift from God was like finding a precious pearl. God had delivered them from a life of bondage and sin.

Many of the Jews were hard-hearted and closed their ears to the Gospel. Some were blinded by Satan's lies. They kept rejecting the preaching of the Word. So Paul and Barnabas had to dust off their feet.

> "But they shook off the dust of their feet against them, and came unto Iconium. And the disciples were filled with joy, and with the Holy Ghost." (Acts 13:51-52)

Joy flows like a river when Jesus sets the captive free. Yet, there is a big danger when people follow the traditions of men and keep rejecting the Lord.

> "And he said unto them, Full well ye reject the commandment of God, that ye may keep your own tradition." (Mark 7:9)

Evil exists with Satan; it is true that Satan incites people to discredit the Gospel of Jesus Christ. He uses all kinds of mediums. We see and hear it by way of the news media, Hollywood, publications, politicians, corrupt leaders, false teachers and pagan traditions. Paul wrote about what happened in the day of Moses. It was real to him—and it's still real today.

"Now as Jannes and Jambres withstood Moses, so do these also resist the truth: men of corrupt minds, reprobate concerning the faith. But they shall proceed no further: for their folly shall be manifest unto all men, as theirs also was.

"But thou hast fully known my doctrine, manner of life, purpose, faith, longsuffering, charity, patience, Persecutions, afflictions, which came unto me at Antioch, at Iconium, at Lystra; what persecutions I endured: but out of them all the Lord delivered me. Yea, and all that will live godly in Christ Jesus shall suffer persecution." (2 Tim. 3:8-12)

The Judaizers were the worst troublemakers throughout Paul's ministry; they were trying to make the Law of Moses equal to the cross. Paul knew the cross fulfilled the law and that keeping the law had no part in our salvation. He knew no one could keep the law. If someone could keep the law, there would be no need for the cross. So, he correctly came against them repeatedly.

Yes! Satan does use people and mediums to work against God. It started with Adam and Eve. There is another big problem with this view of people being the thorn in the flesh—people will not make you humble.

People will cause anger, hate, jealousy, divorce, pride and even murder, as uncontrolled emotions explode into Satan's character.

Is this what Paul was saying when he said, "...lest any man should think of me above that which he seeth me to be, or that he heareth of me. And lest I should be exalted above measure through the abundance of the revelations, there was given to me a thorn in the flesh, the messenger of Satan to buffet me, lest I should be exalted above measure." (2 Cor. 12:6-7)

I can't see the connection—can you? I would say that **people, whether Jew or Gentile,** would have the opposite effect of keeping Paul in measure and humble. It's people who would exalt him.

CONSIDER:

a) If you believe people to be the thorn, then it's time to stop living in the flesh so you won't be bothered by a thorn in the flesh; because God's Word is pricking you to live in Christ.
b) Since Paul lived in Christ, in the Spirit, how could **people** prick the flesh? He lived to please God in the Spirit. No one can please God living in the flesh. The Spirit cannot be pricked. The Spirit is not subject to the flesh. We're not someone's thorn in the flesh.
c) A Nazarene church sign read: **People are not your problem, they are your purpose!** The question is—how do we manage the moment for Christ? We

must move forward in faith and love, regardless of being rejected. Therefore, when the Jews rejected the Gospel, Paul went to the Gentiles. The Gentiles were the heathen or pagans—non-Jews.

"(For he that wrought effectually in Peter to the apostleship of the circumcision, the same was mighty in me toward the Gentiles:)" (Gal. 2:8)

THE BIBLE ANSWERS IT:

a) God desires that all people come to the saving knowledge of Christ. We are to love our neighbors—Gentile and Jew—as ourselves.
b) We are to pray for those who despitefully use us.

People can and will make you angry and get you out of measure. People will cause you to sling mud, fight back, make war and exalt the flesh. People will exalt and worship a president that promotes their views. Oh! But have you read what happened to Herod in the twelfth chapter of the book of Acts?

"And upon a set day Herod, arrayed in royal apparel, sat upon his throne, and made an oration unto them. And the people gave a shout, saying, It is the voice of a god, and not of a man. And immediately the angel of the Lord smote him, because he gave not God the glory: and he was eaten of worms, and gave up the ghost." (Acts 12:21-23)

How can **people** keep you humble and in measure to the love and character of Christ? Paul's thorn in the flesh did.

c) The New Testament confirms that Jesus came to save Jew and Gentile alike. He came for all races.

"There is neither Jew nor Greek, there is neither bond nor free, there is neither male nor female: for ye are all one in Christ Jesus." (Gal. 3:28)

"But I say unto you, Love your enemies, bless them that curse you, do good to them that hate you, and pray for them which despitefully use you, and persecute you; That ye may be the children of your Father which is in heaven: for he maketh his sun to rise on the evil and on the good, and sendeth rain on the just and on the unjust. For if ye love them which love you, what reward have ye? do not even the publicans the same?" (Matt. 5:44-46)

MYTH #2

POOR EYESIGHT AS THE THORN

Some speculate that Paul's thorn was poor eyesight. The Scripture for this is found in three separate places. Paul identifies himself as the author of Romans; yet, Tertius is credited as the writer in Romans 16:22, although in Philemon 19, Paul writes that it was his own hand that was writing Philemon.

> "I Paul have written it with mine own hand, I will repay it: albeit I do not say to thee how thou owest unto me even thine own self besides." (Philemon 19)

My personal comment on this is that I once had 20/20 vision; but when I turned about 40, I had to start wearing eyeglasses. At first I thought it was the green chili that I had added to my diet. It's true! Then I realized that many people start wearing eyeglasses later in life because of focus changes in their eyes. We need spectacles to read and write.

But I don't have poor eyesight; I can read road signs and see to drive in traffic without glasses. Did Isaac have a thorn in the flesh? He couldn't see well enough to recognize Jacob stealing Esau's blessing.

In Gal. 6:11, Paul mentions how large a letter he had written with his own hand. It's possible he needed glasses here too; or, he could be indicating the volume of the book and nothing to do with his eyesight.

An eye problem would have hindered and restricted his preaching the Gospel; but can suffering from something bad and ugly keep you humble?

A number of teachers are trying to link infirmity of the flesh with **poor eyesight;** it is found in the Book of Galatians where Paul wrote about the beginning of his ministry.

> "Ye know how through infirmity of the flesh I preached the gospel unto you at the first. And my temptation which was in my flesh ye despised not, nor rejected; but received me as an angel of God, even as Christ Jesus. Where is then the blessedness ye spake of? for I bear you record, that, if it had been possible, ye would have plucked out your own eyes, and have given them to me." (Gal. 4:13-15)

"Infirmity" has a broad range of meanings as well, and is covered extensively later on in this book. For the moment, though, we are establishing a basis for the many views that people hold to. If we determine to fully understand this passage of Scripture, we need to examine the entire meaning of infirmity to draw a conclusion. As you'll see later, we find he is not talking about himself having poor eyesight to keep him humble, as some interpret this Scripture to mean.

If that were the case, does this mean that because the visions and revelations were so mighty that the Word of God was not sufficient in and of itself to keep Paul humble? Did God have to dim Paul's eyes to cool down his zeal for ministry by turning down his vision to keep him humble? Hasn't the Word with its power to correct behavior been abandoned here?

The Bible teaches that the Word and the Holy Spirit alone were the controllers of Paul's ministry—to direct his life and discern the thoughts and intents of his heart—not dimmed eyes.

> "For the word of God is quick, and powerful, and sharper than any two-edged sword, piercing even to the dividing asunder of soul and spirit, and of the joints and marrow, and is a discerner of the thoughts and intents of the heart." (Heb. 4:12)

There just isn't any Scripture to support this view. Where in the Bible does it show that the saints of God prayed to have **poor eyesight** so that they could be humble like Christ?

MYTH #3

SATAN'S MESSENGER AS THE THORN

Some believe that God permitted Satan to give Paul a demon as the thorn in the flesh—that Satan humbled him. The demon was allegedly assigned to follow Paul around in the ministry to keep him humble. This view would be announcing to the world that Satan didn't want Paul exalted above measure, out of measure, out of bounds; he didn't want Paul to be seen out of character of the Spirit, or out of character to the Holy Word of God; and he didn't want Paul to be heard preaching the Word of God out of the character as an apostle of Jesus Christ. By this, Satan's purpose was to keep Paul humble.

If that were true, then Satan gave Paul the thorn in the flesh because of the wonderful visions and revelations that came from heaven and paradise. It kept the people's eyes on the character of Christ and not on Satan's character. And it kept him from being exalted above measure. Oops—Satan would not want all of that, would he?

Satan doesn't work on purpose to do good will for the Gospel. Satan works to cause doubt and confusion; to usurp God's authority; to deny the deity of Christ; to falsely accuse the believer of not being saved; to tempt a believer (to charm the sin nature), and cause him to fall into sin. He is the defense trial lawyer for the rights of the sin nature. That's him!

One writer put in this way: Satan gave Paul the thorn in the flesh to keep him from receiving more revelations from God.

What a twist of Scripture. This view would be claiming that Satan can intercept God's messages and conversations with a believer and turn them off. That Satan shortened the Bible? What debauchery.

God's communication with a believer is a bloodline that cannot be crossed, wiretapped, interrupted, get a virus, have static, or interference. It's absolutely private. It's clear as crystal. You'll never get a busy signal. There are no dropped calls. There's no power outage. There's no call waiting. You're the first to know what God said. It's free. It's so powerful it can be heard softly and clearly from infinite outer space and its speed is faster than thought. It doesn't have to be approved by the FCC, some denomination, the board of directors, the United Nations or the U.S. Supreme Court. You'll always recognize the voice because the voice always agrees with the Holy Bible. And the voice on the line has never said, "Can you hear me now?"

The instant in-touch number found in the Bible that gives all these options is: PRAYER.

Friend, are you calling now?

"But thou, when thou prayest, enter into thy closet, and when thou hast shut thy door, **pray to thy Father which is in secret**; and **thy Father which seeth in secret** shall reward thee openly." (Matt. 6:6)

"He that dwelleth in the **secret place of the most High** shall abide under the shadow of the Almighty." (Ps. 91:1)

"Daniel answered in the presence of the king, and said, **The secret** which the king hath demanded cannot the wise men, the astrologers, the magicians, the soothsayers, shew unto the king; But there is a God in heaven that revealeth secrets, and maketh known to the king Nebuchadnezzar what shall be in the latter days. Thy dream, and the visions of thy head upon thy bed, are these;" (Dan. 2:27-28)

"But we speak the wisdom of God in a mystery, even the hidden wisdom, which God ordained before the world unto our glory: **Which none of the princes of this world knew:** for had they known it, they would not have crucified the Lord of glory." (1 Cor. 2:7-8)

Once again, another view is immediately refuted because Satan is not privy to God's communication with a believer in Jesus Christ. Satan can't cross over the cross or through the Blood. He is neither omniscient nor omnipotent. He trembles when someone reminds him of the Blood of Jesus. God holds the keys that unlock secrets—not Satan.

Oh! I wonder—could it be possible that the view of Satan's messenger as the thorn in the flesh was initiated by Satan so people would cast off responsibility for their own actions—to suggest they could escape penalty and avoid being accountable for their own sin?

Here are just a few reasons why Satan's messenger is not the thorn in the flesh:

1. God is not in a joint venture with Satan to keep man in measure to the character of Christ.
2. Satan uses the lust of created things to lure a person into pride to exalt the flesh. God gets no pleasure from someone living in the flesh. The flesh is not humble, but proud.
3. **Satan's workshop is the flesh; he works day and night to keep us in the flesh, in sin and out of the measure and character of Christ.**
4. Satan works with all who live for the flesh.

5. Satan tempts the flesh.
6. Satan puffs up the flesh with lust and ego. The flesh goes forth to sow of itself. At harvest time whatever is born of the flesh is flesh. It reaps sinful acts.
7. The flesh is Satan's weapon against God.
8. Temptation is deceitful and subtle to the flesh. "But every man is tempted, when he is drawn away of his own lust, and enticed. Then when lust hath conceived, it bringeth forth sin: and sin, when it is finished, bringeth forth death." (James 1:14-15)
9. The only thing that can prick the flesh (sin nature) is the Word of God.
10. The Spirit rules over the flesh. Praise the Lord!

All things considered, there are people working for Satan who don't know they're doing it. When we speak words of fear and unbelief, those words fall right into the game plan of Satan. Words are powerful tools. If we don't speak words of faith, encouragement, hope and truth, our words may have just scored points for the devil.

Many people are used by Satan simply because they don't know the Word of God. Knowledge of the cross reveals hidden truth.

> "My people are destroyed for lack of knowledge: because thou hast rejected knowledge, I will also reject thee, that thou shalt be no priest to me: seeing

thou hast forgotten the law of thy God, I will also forget thy children." (Hos. 4:6)

"Study to shew thyself approved unto God, a workman that needeth not to be ashamed, rightly dividing the word of truth." (2 Tim. 2:15)

People who have no love for the law of God will be strangers to God. So we need to search His Word to find what is required by God—what the steps are that we must take to have communion and fellowship with a Holy God.

"Thus saith the Lord God; No stranger, uncircumcised in heart, nor uncircumcised in flesh, shall enter into my sanctuary, of any stranger that is among the children of Israel." (Ezek. 44:9)

Fellowship with the Lord is secured by circumcision of the flesh. What kind of messenger are we? Can a believer be an unknowing messenger of Satan? Let us consider what we say: Who will it glorify? Who is talking? When we speak a word to someone, it must be measured by the Word, with the Spirit of God, and not be loose talk that can be considered a message Satan might use.

"Let no corrupt communication proceed out of your mouth, but that which is good to the use of edifying, that it may minister grace unto the hearers.

And grieve not the holy Spirit of God, whereby ye are sealed unto the day of redemption." (Eph. 4:29-30)

"For I say unto you, That except your righteousness shall exceed the righteousness of the scribes and Pharisees, ye shall in no case enter into the kingdom of heaven." (Matt. 5:20)

How do we settle conflicts? Do we point out the law and the written Word, or do we let the law of the Spirit of the life in Christ reconcile it with righteousness by forgiveness and love? A humble servant of Christ will find ways to minister grace to bring glory to Christ. It will require a daily cross. We need to be sure that our words are not those that are unkind from Satan's domain. I repent. I've worked on this one before. Lord, help us respond in love!

"Let the words of my mouth, and the meditation of my heart, be acceptable in thy sight, O Lord, my strength, and my redeemer." (Ps. 19:14)

"The words of a talebearer are as wounds, and they go down into the innermost parts of the belly." (Prov. 18:8)

"Seest thou a man that is hasty in his words? there is more hope of a fool than of him." (Prov. 29:20)

"Be not rash with thy mouth, and let not thine heart be hasty to utter anything before God: for God is in heaven, and thou upon earth: therefore let thy words be few." (Ecc. 5:2)

"Ye have wearied the Lord with your words. Yet ye say, Wherein have we wearied him? When ye say, Everyone that doeth evil is good in the sight of the Lord, and he delighteth in them; or, Where is the God of judgment?" (Mal. 2:17)

"For by thy words thou shalt be justified, and by thy words thou shalt be condemned." (Matt. 12:37)

"Thy words were found, and I did eat them; and thy word was unto me the joy and rejoicing of mine heart: for I am called by thy name, O Lord God of hosts." (Jer. 15:16)

"If thou put the brethren in remembrance of these things, thou shalt be a good minister of Jesus Christ, nourished up in the words of faith and of good doctrine, whereunto thou hast attained." (1 Tim. 4:6)

By understanding the character of Satan and his messenger, we know he absolutely was not the thorn in the flesh. Satan has limited power: **buffeting, accusing, causing doubt**, **blaming others, discrediting** the brethren and/or **influencing your flesh** to get you out of measure and the character of Christ.

"But he giveth more grace. Wherefore he saith, God resisteth the proud, but giveth grace unto the humble.

Submit yourselves therefore to God. Resist the devil, and he will flee from you." (James 4:6-7)

The key steps for believers to get rid of Satan or his messenger are: **submit** to God, quote Scripture, put your flesh on the cross, follow the dictates of the Holy Spirit, practice humility by walking in the Word, resist the devil and **remind** Satan of the following:

1. The cross that Jesus died on.
2. The **blood** Christ shed for you and me.
3. Jesus rose from the dead.
4. The witnesses of Calvary and the resurrection.
5. Satan lost the battle that day at Calvary.
6. God is on the throne—not Satan.
7. The book of Revelation affirms that we win through Christ.
8. Satan cannot cross over the Blood of Christ.
9. We have the new covenant—the New Testament.
10. Jesus has been given all power.
11. Jesus is Lord!

THE DAY THE ACCUSER OF THE BRETHREN IS DISARMED

"And I heard a loud voice saying in heaven, Now is come salvation, and strength, and the kingdom of our

God, and the power of his Christ: **for the accuser of our brethren is cast down**, which accused them before our God day and night. **And they overcame him by the blood of the Lamb, and by the word of their testimony**; and they loved not their lives unto the death." (Rev. 2:10-11)

"Be strong and courageous, be not afraid nor dismayed for the king of Assyria, nor for all the multitude that is with him: for there be more with us than with him: With him is an arm of flesh; but with us is the LORD our God to help us, and to fight our battles. And the people rested themselves upon the words of Hezekiah king of Judah." (2 Chron. 32:7-8)

"For the grace of God that bringeth salvation hath appeared to all men, Teaching us that, denying ungodliness and worldly lusts, we should live soberly, righteously, and godly, in this present world; Looking for that blessed hope, and the glorious appearing of the great God and our Saviour Jesus Christ; Who gave himself for us, that he might redeem us from all iniquity, and purify unto himself a peculiar people, zealous of good works." (Titus 2:11-14)

According to the Word of God, the devil's days are numbered. There is coming a day when he will no longer deceive the nations.

"And he laid hold on the dragon, that old serpent, which is the Devil, and Satan, and bound him a thousand years, And cast him into the bottomless pit, and shut him up, and set a seal upon him, that he should deceive the nations no more, till the thousand years should be fulfilled: and after that he must be loosed a little season." (Rev. 20:2-3)

Now that Satan and his messenger are exposed by the Word, we need to set our spiritual compass on things above. We must turn our hearts toward home.

"And I John saw the holy city, new Jerusalem, coming down from God out of heaven, prepared as a bride adorned for her husband." (Rev. 21:2)

WHAT IS HEAVEN LIKE?

A preacher once said, *"We don't know how to fully describe heaven because it has not been totally revealed to us; but we know some of what we have down here will not be in heaven. For instance, there will be no curse, no more suffering, no more pain, no sickness, no disease, no death, no orphans, no handicapped people, no blindness, no loneliness, no sadness, no despair, no strife, no arguments, no aborted babies, no bankruptcies, no fraud, no stealing, no identify theft, no divorce, no terror, no fear, and no crisis."*

It sounds like the place where we would all like to live forever—doesn't it? It sounds like home to me.

"And he shewed me a pure river of water of life, clear as crystal, proceeding out of the throne of God and of the Lamb. In the midst of the street of it, and on either side of the river, was there the tree of life, which bare twelve manner of fruits, and yielded her fruit every month: and the leaves of the tree were for the healing of the nations. And there shall be no more curse: but the throne of God and of the Lamb shall be in it; and his servants shall serve him:" (Rev. 22:1-3)

At a funeral recently the preacher said, *"This man you have come to pay your last respects to was a born again Christian. He found Christ as Savior. He repented of sin, invited Jesus Christ into his heart and walked with God. The only way you will get to see him again is do what he did and invite Jesus Christ into your heart. There is a heaven to gain and a hell to shun. If you have done what he did—**it is see you later**. If you have not; well, then, sadly this is the day and moment to say good bye forever."*

At the end of time on earth the greatest word we will ever hear is "Come." The Spirit and the bride will say, "Come." So come, Lord Jesus, come. We long to see your face and behold your glory.

> "And the Spirit and the bride say, Come. And let him that heareth say, Come. And let him that is athirst come. And whosoever will, let him take the water of life freely." (Rev. 22:17)

MYTH #4

THE THORN LEFT UNKNOWN SO YOU COULD CHOOSE YOUR OWN

Recent comments by some authors say that the thorn in the flesh was purposely left unknown by God—reason being, you could name your own thorn.

This idea has probably surfaced because there are things we don't have full control over in our lives. Some people have experienced physical limits which they have no power over, so they blame it on the thorn in the flesh.

Some suggest that handicapped people have a thorn in the flesh because they are not healed. Okay, a stomach ache, motion sickness, bone spurs and headaches would fit, too. Yet, could anyone with a physical limitation still throw a flesh fit, using bad words or acting ugly, **and be exalted above measure**?

By this view, the Word is powerless to convict of sin if their character is **seen or heard exalted above measure**. They might be restricted or humbled by their physical condition, but that is all.

Aren't most of these views just opinions? Where is the Scripture reference to support it? Some can only imply that God didn't heal Paul of the unknown thorn.

If it's open for sinners to name their own thorn, it would be a serious contradiction of Scripture. God's Word would be corrupt because it would void the Blood of Jesus Christ. It would be an excuse for sinners to blame a weakness or sin on their thorn. The Word that was written to admonish or convict of sin would be made ineffective.

If the **unknown** were any **physical blemish or personal failure,** the thorn in the flesh could take on a life of its own. It would constantly remind of some weakness in the flesh or sin that happened in the past. Then guilt is not eradicated by the Blood of Christ, the cross, sanctification and the promises of God. The devil would accuse day and night of an ugly past sin once committed while trying to satisfy the cry of the flesh.

> "For all have sinned, and come short of the glory of God;" (Rom. 3:23)

Satan would be free to promote doubt of the forgiveness of God. But hold on! We have good news: we have victory through the cross, and the Word which contradicts that wrong view by Scriptures that are able to remove all guilt and bring physical health to set the captive free.

> "Be not wise in thine own eyes: fear the LORD, and depart from evil. It shall be health to thy navel, and marrow to thy bones." (Prov. 3:7-8)
>
> "Come now, and let us reason together, saith the LORD: though your sins be as scarlet, they shall be as white as snow; though they be red like crimson, they shall be as wool." (Isa. 1:18)

Therefore, the first thing to do with sin is to repent, make restitution and walk in the Word. Look at the cross and what Jesus did for us there. Stop living for the flesh.

> "Remember therefore from whence thou art fallen, and repent, and do the first works; or else I will come unto thee quickly, and will remove thy candlestick out of his place, except thou repent." (Rev. 2:5)

The Blood of Jesus Christ redeems us from all our sin. His cleansing power was complete at **the cross**. The resurrection proves that He lives to make intercession for us as our mediator.

> "Saying, Blessed are they whose iniquities are forgiven, and whose sins are covered. Blessed is the man to whom the Lord will not impute sin." (Rom. 4:7-8)

Some are quick to give an off-the-cuff, shoot-from-the-hip answer to a topic that is very deep and complicated. Many rely upon hearsay or say something from a commentary without prayer and deep research. These first responders to a Bible topic are subject to error. The Holy Spirit is the only source to validate the Word.

I've listened to many good pastors and teachers talk about what they think the thorn in the flesh was. Yet, none have ever pointed to the fact and truth that the thorn kept Paul in the Word—in character—and in the measure of the Word. If he ever got exalted above the Word, he would have been out of character to the Word, and ineffective. Fact is—who has given more than a one-liner for their view?

I could list the titles of books and authors that support these views, but that would not advance the kingdom of God. I would not want to discredit other good works many of these servants of God have done.

Isn't the Bible too complex for one to explain satisfactorily by just using a commentary? A believer's heart and mind can only be opened to deep truth by revelation coming from the Holy Spirit. Truth is not an opinion. God is not the author of speculation. Is not doubt and misinformation the state of confusion that Satan wants everyone in? Who would attend a Bible class that taught speculation?

Today, we have specialists in all fields of service, especially in health care. If we have pain in our feet, we don't go to a dentist or an ophthalmologist, we go to a podiatrist. The body in need of serious examination is too complex for a general practitioner. Don't you sometimes cringe that doctors are just practicing? Jesus does not practice.

No one knows the whole counsel of the Word of God. Some things we do not understand must be left under the Blood. Yet, what will withstand any examination as truth is the Word of God that points all people to the saving knowledge of Jesus Christ and the cross.

> An old preacher once said, "You can listen to almost any preacher, and whatever is bothering him, that's his thorn in the flesh."

One preacher said that while he was preaching in the dead heat of the south, the air conditioner went out in the church. He said it was his thorn in the flesh. Where does his view connect to the Word or the Spirit? Isn't he saying that whatever is an inconvenience is a thorn in the flesh?

I would say to him, "Stop living in the weakness of the flesh and live more in the Spirit to please the Lord." The Spirit is ready to take authority over any situation in your life, especially at that moment when something goes wrong.

Also, avoid all businesses, conversations and establishments that promote the temptation of the sin nature (flesh).

In current times, some claim abominable sexual desires as their thorn in the flesh. A few have expressed hope for a future where one can "be who you are" and be accepted and loved in the Christian community. Some speak about separating some of the teaching of Scripture. Jesus is accepted, but Paul's writings are rejected. Does this not sound like the character of Sodom and Gomorrha?

> "Even as Sodom and Gomorrha, and the cities about them in like manner, giving themselves over to fornication, and going after strange flesh, are set forth for an example, suffering the vengeance of eternal fire." (Jude 7)

We know by Scripture what is not acceptable; but some want freedom to do whatever pleases them, casting aside whatever doesn't suit them. The deception here is real, and Satan is the one that deceives them. Some accept, as truth, only the words of the Bible that are written in red. If they disagree with the apostle Paul, then they disagree with Jesus Christ, because Paul represents the Lord Jesus Christ in all his writings. It's the Word.

> "Of how much sorer punishment, suppose ye, shall he be thought worthy, who hath trodden underfoot

the Son of God, and hath counted the blood of the covenant, wherewith he was sanctified, an unholy thing, and hath done despite unto the Spirit of grace?" (Heb. 10:29)

In the Middle East there is a boiling **hate** in the minds and hearts of millions of people. Satan has deceived them. The Bible says he who hates his brother will not have eternal life. Yet, you can't love your brother if you don't know the Father; and you can't know the Father if you don't know the Son.

"Whosoever denieth the Son, the same hath not the Father: (but) he that acknowledgeth the Son hath the Father also." (1 John 2:23)

"All things are delivered unto me of my Father: and no man knoweth the Son, but the Father; neither knoweth any man the Father, save the Son, and he to whomsoever the Son will reveal him." (Matt 11:27)

"He that loveth not knoweth not God; for God is love." (1 John 4:8)

"And be ye kind one to another, tenderhearted, forgiving one another, even as God for Christ's sake hath forgiven you." (Eph. 4:32)

"**And ye are complete in him**, which is the head of all principality and power: In whom also ye are circumcised with the circumcision made without hands, in putting off the body of the sins of the flesh by the circumcision of Christ: Buried with him in baptism, wherein also ye are risen with him through the faith of the operation of God, who hath raised him from the dead.

"And you, being dead in your sins and the uncircumcision of your flesh, hath he quickened together with him, having forgiven you all trespasses; **Blotting out the handwriting of ordinances that was against us, which was contrary to us, and took it out of the way, nailing it to his cross;** And having spoiled principalities and powers, he made a shew of them openly, triumphing over them in it." (Col. 2:10-15)

Jesus took the law of sin and death (sin nature) and nailed it to the cross. Thus, Satan lost his legal right to hold man in bondage. Glory to Christ our Lord! Now all we need to do is look at the cross that gave us Amazing Grace and victory. There are innumerable promises in the Word of God that will disarm any accusation the enemy might use to discredit our testimony and our forgiveness from sin. We rest in victory over sin through the cross. The Word gives us power to overcome sin.

"Ye are of God, little children, and have overcome them: because greater is he that is in you, than he that is in the world." (1 John 4:4)

"If ye then be risen with Christ, seek those things which are above, where Christ sitteth on the right hand of God. Set your affection on things above, not on things on the earth. For ye are dead, and your life is hid with Christ in God. When Christ, who is our life, shall appear, then shall ye also appear with him in glory.

"Mortify therefore your members which are upon the earth; fornication, uncleanness, inordinate affection, evil concupiscence, and covetousness, which is idolatry: For which things' sake the wrath of God cometh on the children of disobedience: In the which ye also walked some time, when ye lived in them.

"But now ye also put off all these; anger, wrath, malice, blasphemy, filthy communication out of your mouth. Lie not one to another, seeing that ye have put off the old man with his deeds; And have put on the new man, which is renewed in knowledge after the image of him that created him: Where there is neither Greek nor Jew, circumcision nor uncircumcision, Barbarian, Scythian, bond nor free: but Christ is all, and in all." (Col. 3:1-11)

"That I may know him, and the power of his resurrection, and the fellowship of his sufferings, being made conformable unto his death; If by any means I might attain unto the resurrection of the dead. Not as though I had already attained, either were already perfect: but I follow after, if that I may apprehend that for which also I am apprehended of Christ Jesus.

"Brethren, I count not myself to have apprehended: but this one thing I do, forgetting those things which are behind, and reaching forth unto those things which are before, I press toward the mark for the prize of the high calling of God in Christ Jesus." (Phil. 3:10-14)

All of the above Scriptures discredit a **personal failure, or "name your own thorn"** as being the thorn in the flesh. The Word is greater than any of our failures in the flesh. The Word never bows down to a failure and says, "You win." For God has cast all of our sins and failures into the sea of forgetfulness. When God looks at us, He can only see **the Blood**. Yes! Jesus Christ cleansed us from all sin and unrighteousness. For Jesus' Blood redeemed us, and His Word washed away the record of sin that was written against us. We are made perfect in Him and have His testimony of faith, hope and victory by the cross. He changed our will to His will.

"As far as the east is from the west, so far hath he removed our transgressions from us." (Ps. 103:12)

"Like as a father pitieth his children, so the LORD pitieth them that fear him. For he knoweth our frame; he remembereth that we are dust." (Ps. 103:13-14)

"Fear thou not; for I am with thee: be not dismayed; for I am thy God: I will strengthen thee; yea, I will help thee; yea, I will uphold thee with the right hand of my righteousness." (Isa. 41:10)

"And, having made peace through the blood of his cross, by him to reconcile all things unto himself; by him, I say, whether they be things in earth, or things in heaven. And you, that were sometime alienated and enemies in your mind by wicked works, yet now hath he reconciled. In the body of his flesh through death, to present you holy and unblameable and unreproveable in his sight:" (Col. 1:20-22)

"Take heed, brethren, lest there be in any of you an evil heart of unbelief, in departing from the living God." (Heb. 3:12)

"But if we walk in the light, as he is in the light, we have fellowship one with another, and the blood of Jesus Christ his Son cleanseth us from all sin." (1 John 1:7)

What a wonderful comfort and peace to know our sins are forgiven and that God is **not** keeping a record of our past failures. He sees us as perfect and pure through the Blood. The Blood of Jesus Christ built the bridge that gives us fellowship with God. The Blood of Jesus Christ removes all stains of sinful acts of the flesh. We're Blood-bought in Christ.

"Not that I speak in respect of want: for I have learned, in whatsoever state I am, therewith to be content." (Phil. 4:11)

All of the views mentioned by spiritual leaders say Paul's thorn was some kind of problem that God would not heal or remove by prayer. It is at this point we get into doctrinal issues:

1. Some churches and denominations embrace any view as long as it doesn't conflict with their church doctrine. For instance, the Pentecostals believe in divine healing, so none of the views that pertain to a physical problem are considered. They believe that many times physical problems can be resolved by prayer, supported by using faith and healing Scriptures. Thus, most point to the Judaizers as Paul's thorn in the flesh.
2. Those churches who don't believe in divine healing find it reasonable to embrace some physical problem: poor eyesight with ophthalmia being the problem, epilepsy, a birthmark, motion sickness, headaches, stomach weakness, a speech impediment, being handicapped, any physical disorder or the unknown—just stake a claim to your own thorn.

However, because of unsatisfied logic or proof of Scripture to any of these views, many pastors and teachers conclude it was an unknown infirmity.

MYTH #5

INFIRMITY VIEW AS THE THORN

Infirmity is the view that writers of commentaries end up hanging their hat on. Infirmity has broad implications and everyone is touched by it. But isn't this just trying to put the blame on something?

Barnes Notes declares that most of the views we've already mentioned as the thorn in the flesh are vain and ridiculous, although he does conclude that it was some infirmity of the flesh, as follows:

But all conjecture here is vain; and the numerous strange and ridiculous opinions of commentators is a melancholy attestation of their inclination to fanciful conjecture where it is impossible in the nature of the case to ascertain the truth. All that can be known of this is that it was some infirmity of the flesh, some bodily affliction or calamity, that was like the continual piercing of the flesh with a thorn (Gal. 4:13);

and that it was something that was designed to prevent spiritual pride. It is not indeed an improbable supposition that it was something that could be seen by others, and that it thus tended to humble him when he was with them.

(from Barnes' Notes, Electronic Database. Copyright (c) 1997 by Biblesoft)

Barnes eliminates all but infirmity as being the thorn in the flesh; but as you will see later in this book—Scripture proves all people have an infirmity. Can we therefore say all people are naturally humble?

To help expedite a point, let's suppose for a moment that infirmity was Paul's thorn and what the day might be like for Paul:

Paul speaking, "After breakfast the first thing I do is think about the revelations that God has given me; I immediately feel **infirmity** awaken my emotions, so I quickly humble myself so no one will see or hear me exalted above measure.

"Then when I stand preaching the Word of God, everyone knows that the revelations God has revealed to me are so mighty that God has to give me an infirmity of the flesh, a kind of malfunction of the flesh. It is an unknown thing that pricks my flesh to show others how humble I am.

"Many that hear my gospel see the miracles that follow me (you know, the signs and wonders) and want to be just like me; so as I limp over to the podium, I begin telling them to follow me as I follow Christ; but some are afraid they might get the **infirmity** too; so I have to encourage them that God has not given us the spirit of fear; but of power, and of love, and of a sound mind.

"Yet, a few have stopped attending my meetings because of doubt and unbelief. But we know that many who see and hear my preaching know that God is only showing them that infirmity is God's secret weapon to rid the flesh of pride, and it causes all to know how to live humbly like me.

"And by the way, I want all to know that none of these things bother me because I labor more abundantly than them all: I've had stripes above measure; I was in prison more frequent; in deaths oft, of the Jews five times received thirty-nine stripes. Three times beaten with rods; once stoned and suffered shipwreck.

"Therefore, I ask you to seek infirmity for yourself so that you can have the character of humility like me. You'll get used to the physical problem that no one knows. Trust me. It's for your own good."

It would really be a reach to agree with this view. It just doesn't fit the Gospel. It is not the curse that came because of sin that was the thorn in the flesh to keep Paul in measure.

The law of the Spirit of life in Christ in you and me breaks the curse of sin. We are washed by the Blood and are no longer under the curse.

"But that no man is justified by the law in the sight of God, it is evident: for, The just shall live by faith. And

> the law is not of faith: but, The man that doeth them shall live in them. **Christ hath redeemed us from the curse of the law, being made a curse for us: for it is written, Cursed is every one that hangeth on a tree:"** (Gal. 3:11-13)

Without the law, we would not know there is a breach between sin and righteousness. It stands by ready to punish the guilty. It only wields judgment. The law has **no mercy, grace, or love**. A blind man standing in a no-parking zone, waiting in the wind and rain for a taxi with his pregnant wife, about to give birth to twins, would be given a citation. The law has no compassion. Christ came to free us from the condemnation of the law. We are justified in the righteousness of Christ.

No one can blame our human imperfections on the thorn in the flesh. We were all made by God to take responsibility for our own actions and live in Christ to the glory of God.

You will be excited to learn that Paul's thorn in the flesh gave him amazing insight into the glorious Gospel.

> "Verily, verily, I say unto you, He that believeth on me, the works that I do shall he do also; and greater works than these shall he do; because I go unto my Father." (John 14:12)

God doesn't owe us anything. He has given us life. It is not in the physical realm that we serve him—it is in the spiritual realm. If all we can do is breathe the name of Jesus, it serves a purpose for God.

> "For if there be first a willing mind, it is accepted according to that a man hath, and not according to that he hath not." (2 Cor. 8:12)

Go ask the blind man if his lack of vision or sight works to keep him humble. He will tell you the blind, as well, need the convicting power of the Holy Spirit to reveal the sin in their heart. The blind are no different than sighted people. They too need to repent of sin to experience the saving knowledge and transforming power of Jesus Christ.

A comparison can be made of the woman caught in adultery and brought before Jesus by her accusers. They quoted the Law of Moses that condemned her to death. Jesus stooped down and began writing with his finger on the ground. When they continued on the subject he stood up and said, "He that is without sin cast the first stone." Then He stooped down and continued to write:

> "And they which heard it, being convicted by their own conscience, went out one by one, beginning at the eldest, even unto the last: and Jesus was left alone, and the woman standing in the midst.

"When Jesus had lifted up himself, and saw none but the woman, he said unto her, Woman, where are those thine accusers? hath no man condemned thee? She said, No man, Lord. And Jesus said unto her, Neither do I condemn thee: go, and sin no more." (John 8:9-11)

Some Biblical scholars have conflicting views and speculate as to what the words were that Jesus wrote in the sand. Did you notice the words had **the power to convict them of sin?** What words would do that? Did Jesus perhaps write some of the Ten Commandments in the sand, like God wrote in stone the rules to govern the nation of Israel for Moses on Mount Sinai?

This is the reason some people are using our courts to fight against the Ten Commandments, seeking to remove them from public display and awareness, so their lifestyle will be uninhibited. Where there is no moral compass, there is no truth!

THE TEN COMMANDMENTS

1. **I am the Lord thy God and thou shalt not have other gods besides me.**
2. **Thou shalt not make for thyself any graven image.**
3. **Thou shalt not take the name of the Lord thy God in vain.**

4. Remember the Lord's Day to keep it holy.
5. Honor thy Father and Mother.
6. Thou shalt not kill.
7. Thou shalt not commit adultery.
8. Thou shalt not steal.
9. Thou shalt not bear false witness against thy neighbor.
10. Thou shalt not covet.

Who can throw a stone when we examine our own hearts by God's law?

> "Now we know that what things soever the law saith, it saith to them who are under the law: that every mouth may be stopped, and all the world may become guilty before God." (Rom 3:19)
>
> "Therefore by the deeds of the law there shall no flesh be justified in his sight: for by the law is the knowledge of sin." (Rom. 3:20)

There it is! Not one accuser was justified, for there is at least one of the Ten Commandments that all people have broken and that is: "thou shalt not covet." Who among us or the accusers have never coveted something? Not one! Only Jesus has lived a perfect life.

"What shall we say then? Is the law sin? God forbid. Nay, I had not known sin, but by the law: for I had not known lust, except the law had said, Thou shalt not covet." (Rom 7:7)

The knowledge of sin is revealed to all. We were not offended until we learned the law. The law convicted us and brought us to Christ.

"But when the fullness of the time was come, God sent forth his Son, made of a woman, made under the law, To redeem them that were under the law, that we might receive the adoption of sons." (Gal 4:4-5)

Therefore, anyone that thinks **the law** or **the flesh** (including other people's flesh) was used in any way to keep Paul in measure of the Gospel as the thorn in the flesh, does not understand the character of God.

"For sin shall not have dominion over you: for ye are not under the law, but under grace. What then? shall we sin, because we are not under the law, but under grace? God forbid." (Rom 6:14-15)

Therefore, having faith in Jesus Christ and the cross is God's promise to the believer of a full pardon and **unmerited grace**. Paul ends all of his Epistles with grace.

God has made known to us His plan of salvation in ingenious ways, so that we have no excuse and so that we can better understand His Holy character and nature. He brings it to the attention of the world in dazzling ways, so that we can easily remember the historical account of the cross that points us to being justified by faith.

EXAMPLES:

1. Noah building the ark is a type and shadow of salvation.
2. Abraham offered his son Isaac as a sacrifice to God, and God provided a ram.
3. Esau sold his birthright to Jacob.
4. Joseph sold as a slave by his own brothers; then his dreams came to pass when his brothers came to Egypt to buy grain. His life was a picture of Christ as Savior for Israel.
5. Moses, when just a baby, was placed in an ark of bulrushes to escape death—was found by Pharaoh's daughter, who summoned a maid to find a nurse to care for him—the nurse turned out to be his own mother! He cares for us.
6. David, as a boy, killed the giant Goliath with a slingshot and later became king of Judah and Israel. Jesus is our King from the seed of David.

7. Jonah, the unforgiving preacher, ran from the call of God and spent three days and three nights in the belly of a great fish. Christ was in the grave three days.
8. Zacharias, because of unbelief, was struck dumb. Then, after the child was born, when asked the name of the child, he motioned for a writing table and wrote "John." Immediately his tongue was loosed and he spoke and praised God. It is here we learn that the unbeliever is dumb and has nothing to say. John the Baptist was the forerunner of Christ.
9. Mary, a virgin, gave birth to Jesus Christ, who was born without the sin nature.
10. John the Baptist, when he said, "Behold the Lamb of God that takes away the sin of the world."
11. Jesus nailed to a cross for our sin.
12. The day of Pentecost and the dramatic appearing of the Holy Spirit in cloven (to adhere, cleave, be faithful) tongues like as of fire. He came to abide with believers in Christ and assist them through spiritual gifts.
13. The prodigal son as a type of salvation, when in the pig pen he came to his senses. He acknowledged his sin (sin nature) and returned to his father.
14. Saul blinded by a great light and saved on the road to Damascus. Three days later he was healed and filled with the Holy Ghost when God instructed Ananias to put his hands on him. The Lord used this man, Paul,

to write the way **to live without condemnation of sin**. Here is how it began:

"And as he journeyed, he came near Damascus: and suddenly there shined round about him a light from heaven:" (Acts 9:3)

"And Saul arose from the earth; and when his eyes were opened, he saw no man: but they led him by the hand, and brought him into Damascus. And he was three days without sight, and neither did eat nor drink." (Acts 9:8-9)

"And there was a certain disciple at Damascus, named Ananias; and to him said the Lord in a vision, Ananias. And he said, Behold, I am here, Lord. And the Lord said unto him, Arise, and go into the street which is called Straight, and inquire in the house of Judas for one called Saul, of Tarsus: for, behold, he prayeth, And hath seen in a vision a man named Ananias coming in, and putting his hand on him, that he might receive his sight." (Acts 9:10-12)

When Saul got healed of his blindness and filled with the Holy Ghost, it was Jesus who sent Ananias to do the official work of the ministry. We see this over and over in the Bible; how the Lord uses someone He has already qualified to administer His spiritual work. What a blessing was awarded Ananias to be a part of the birth of the Lord's great work.

"And Ananias went his way, and entered into the house; and putting his hands on him said, Brother Saul, the Lord, even Jesus, that appeared unto thee in the way as thou camest, hath sent me, **that thou mightest receive thy sight, and be filled with the Holy Ghost.**

"**And immediately there fell from his eyes as it had been scales: and he received sight forthwith,** and arose, and was baptized. And when he had received meat, he was strengthened. Then was Saul certain days with the disciples which were at Damascus. (Acts 9:17-19)

Would God have given Paul poor eyesight when the scales fell off? If so, did he receive a poor infilling of the Holy Spirit also?

"And straightway he preached Christ in the synagogues, that he is the Son of God." (Acts 9:20)

Meeting Jesus on the road to Damascus changed Saul forever. His birth name Saul is changed to Paul. In Hebrew, Paul means extraordinary and wonderful.

"Then Saul, (who also is called Paul,) filled with the Holy Ghost, set his eyes on him," (Acts 13:9)

Here is where his eyes were focused on a false prophet, a Jew, whose name was Bar-jesus; it was early in Paul's ministry when he was still mostly known as Saul. Saul became known as Paul later on.

Did you ever wonder what kept Paul preaching the Gospel after all that came against him? Look at the following from 2 Cor. 11:23-27:

1. In labors more abundant.
2. In stripes above measure.
3. In prison more frequent.
4. In death often.
5. Of the Jews five times received thirty-nine stripes.
6. Three times beaten with rods.
7. Once stoned.
8. Suffered shipwreck.
9. A day and a night in the deep.
10. In perils of waters.
11. In perils of robbers.
12. In perils by my own countrymen.
13. In perils by the heathen.
14. In perils in the city.
15. In perils in the wilderness.
16. In perils in the sea.
17. In perils among false brethren.
18. In weariness and painfulness.

19. In watching often, in hunger and thirst, in fasting often.
20. In cold and nakedness.

Why didn't he just throw in the towel and say "I quit" like many have done? What kept him focused and determined to finish the race? What was inside this man that made him abound in the things of God? What would make the mission of God so worthy and clear that no one could sway him off course or change his profession (like tempting him with silver and gold into selling numbers at a camel race, or making tents to sell for consumers at Jerusalem-mart) instead of preaching the Gospel?

It was the call of God engraved upon Paul's heart, mind and soul that revealed to him the will of God and its purpose. **The call** was the only thing that would keep him in pursuit of fulfilling the mission.

It was the vision and revelation from Almighty God that showed him the glorious message of the cross and future salvation of souls. He knew he had a mission that was glorious in the redemption of lost souls. It was getting people trained as ministers of the Gospel of Jesus Christ. He lived the Gospel to show all saints how to use **spiritual tools**.

Paul also knew he must fight against Satan and his messenger to keep the faith and win the battle over Satan and the flesh that wars against the Spirit.

"For though I would desire to glory, I shall not be a fool; for I will say the truth: but now I forbear, lest any man should think of me above that which he seeth me to be, or that he heareth of me. And lest I should be exalted above measure through the abundance of the revelations, there was given to me a thorn in the flesh, the messenger of Satan to buffet me, lest I should be exalted above measure." (2 Cor. 12:6-7)

Paul was saying that the thorn in the flesh kept him on course, in measure to the visions and revelations of the Lord. Its purpose was multi-dimensional. It was God-designed to control behavior becoming of the character of the Word. How would **people** or **poor eyesight** do all that?

Some connect the eye problem with ophthalmia. By this, Paul's eyes would swell into disfigurement and be very painful. Others think Paul had been bitten by a mosquito and contacted malaria showing intermittent or recurring symptoms of chills, fever and sweating. Therefore, in theory to this view: Paul would be preaching in one of his crusades and a mosquito would fly by his nose; sensing the coming chills, fever and sweating, he would go into a humble mode.

Don't we know that if Paul can shake off a deadly snake and feel no harm, he certainly can swat a mosquito in Jesus' name?

> "Who shall separate us from the love of Christ? shall tribulation, or distress, or persecution, or famine, or nakedness, or peril, or sword? As it is written, For thy sake we are killed all the daylong; we are accounted as sheep for the slaughter. Nay, in all these things we are more than conquerors through him that loved us." (Rom. 8:35-37)

There are many perils and dangers in life; but we know our steps are ordered by the Lord when we obey the Word. His healing presence keeps us safe. We just need to live by faith, do the works of an evangelist, and let God do the rest.

> "Confess your faults one to another, and pray one for another, that ye may be healed. The effectual fervent prayer of a righteous man availeth much." (James 5:16)

MYTH #6

PHYSICAL LIMITATIONS

GOOD NEWS: After showing the views that many biblical scholars, teachers and pastors have concluded as the source to keep Paul humble, the following Scriptures prove that physical limitations and problems of the flesh cannot be Paul's thorn in the flesh.

> "A son honoureth his father, and a servant his master: if then I be a father, where is mine honour? and if I be a master, where is my fear? saith the LORD of hosts unto you, O priests, that despise my name. And ye say, Wherein have we despised thy name?
>
> "Ye offer polluted bread upon mine altar; and ye say, Wherein have we polluted thee? In that ye say, The table of the LORD is contemptible.
>
> "And if ye offer the blind for sacrifice, is it not evil? and if ye offer the lame and sick, is it not evil?

offer it now unto thy governor; will he be pleased with thee, or accept thy person? saith the LORD of hosts." (Mal. 1:6-8)

As years passed, so did the lack of adherence to the Law of Moses. For many, it was just a religious ritual with no value or meaning. God's commandments as to how sacrifices were to be carried out became tainted.

"And this is the thing that thou shalt do unto them to hallow them, to minister unto me in the priest's office: Take one young bullock, and two rams without blemish," (Ex. 29:1)

The holiness of God for the office of priesthood is established here. The position of service was to be holy and **unblemished**. However, the priests got caught in evil deception, leaving God's purpose of an unblemished sacrifice. The priests were trying to upgrade their livestock by culling out the blind, lame and sick—offering them to God for the sacrifice of sin, since the animal had an eye disease, limped or was nearly dead anyway. Knowing that they were commanded to sacrifice an animal for sin, why not offer the blemished one?

"If the priest that is anointed do sin according to the sin of the people; then let him bring for his sin, which he hath sinned, a young bullock **without blemish** unto the LORD for a sin offering." (Lev. 4:3)

The thorn in the flesh kept Paul in measure of the Word. We know that humility is not one of the devil's characteristics. Humility is a trademark belonging to God's character and was perfectly portrayed at the cross. It is very useful to the believer who yields to spiritual control. One reason the thorn was given was so that no one could point a finger at Paul and say, "Hey Paul! You're out of the character of Christ, the Holy Word of God, you're exalted above measure." Paul knew something about being beyond measure from his past.

"For ye have heard of my conversation in time past in the Jews' religion, how that beyond measure I persecuted the church of God, and wasted it:" (Gal. 1:13)

THE SECRET IS IN THE WORD MEASURE

Truth is, when you bake a cake, you must put together the correct measure of ingredients: flour, sugar, milk, baking soda, flavoring, shortening and eggs. If you leave out one of these main ingredients, you will not end up with a good cake. By comparison, the word **measure** is very important in the study of the thorn in the flesh.

Webster says measure means a fixed or suitable limit; the dimensions, capacity or amount of something ascertained by measuring; an estimate of what is to be expected (as of a person or situation). It's what we use to measure everything we do. It's cadence; it's musical time; it's the basis for comparison. We measure out money to buy or sell.

Notably, it's the limit or boundary in character and purpose that makes an apostle: **first** is the call from God; **second** is the purpose of the call, which is the message of the Gospel of Jesus Christ; **third** is the character of the call. None of these can be above measure, out of measure or missing, to be seen and heard as an apostleship of Jesus Christ. The most important use of measure concerning the Word or Christ is that **it cannot be blemished**.

For this reason alone, all of us need the boundary; the measure of the Gospel of Jesus Christ. Are we of its DNA? The measure of our faith is Jesus Christ and the crucifixion. Without the Blood, there is no remission of sin. We must live by faith in Christ and abide in **measure** to the character of Christ. As believers, we must stay in measure (in bounds to the Gospel) to what God has called us to live as Christians and as examples to the world.

Look at all the games in sports that have boundaries: baseball, football, soccer, golf, racing, etc. Believers play by the rules, too. John 16:13 shows the Christian's referee is the Holy Spirit.

Now, considering the Scripture that's been given, with all of the above, we clearly see **people** or **poor eyesight** couldn't be a possible source to keep someone in measure of the character of Christ. It is not comparable to what the pure Word of God does in keeping us from being exalted above measure. The character of Christ must be our heart and soul. When we read the Word, it convicts; it has power to bring change.

> "And these things, brethren, I have in a figure transferred to myself and to Apollos for your sakes; that

ye might learn in us not to think of men above that which is written, that no one of you be puffed up for one against another." (1 Cor. 4:6)

On earth we wear a costume of flesh, and there is just no way we can get it saved and into heaven; so why are so many people trying to do it? It can't be redeemed or shed from us until death. On that day—we get our new glorious resurrected body!

Until then, do this: Take off the old sin nature and put on the new. The old nature must remain in our prayer closet as a worn-out, color-faded, filthy rag-torn garment spotted with flesh. It's that old man we don't wear anymore. We are now a new man in Christ. We wear the robe of righteousness in Christ. In Christ we have a changed life, and our new duds make us look and act like a king's kid!

"And that ye put on the new man, which after God is created in righteousness and true holiness." (Eph. 4:24)

"That no flesh glory in his presence. But of him are ye in Christ Jesus, who of God is made unto us wisdom, and righteousness, and sanctification, and redemption: That, according as it is written, He that glorieth, let him glory in the Lord." (1 Cor. 1:29-31)

To the believer in Christ, the only way to become humble and stay in measure to the call and revelation of God is by the transforming power of the Holy Spirit. There is nothing in the physical realm (the flesh) that has power to cause one to be humble. It is having a constant awareness that we are to live in the spirit, in Christ, according to the Holy Word of God.

> "Likewise, ye younger, submit yourselves unto the elder. Yea, all of you be subject one to another, and be clothed with humility: for God resisteth the proud, and giveth grace to the humble. Humble yourselves therefore under the mighty hand of God, that he may exalt you in due time:" (1 Peter 5:6)

Paul uses the word "humble" only one time in all of his writings—in reference to his fear and concern of learning that his converts have not repented of horrible sin.

> "For I fear, lest, when I come, I shall not find you such as I would, and that I shall be found unto you such as ye would not: lest there be debates, envyings, wraths, strifes, backbitings, whisperings, swellings, tumults: And lest, when I come again, my God will humble me among you, and that I shall bewail many which have sinned already, and have not repented of

> the uncleanness and fornication and lasciviousness which they have committed." (2 Cor. 12:20-21)

Paul had concerns that his converts would stray from the message of the cross. The Old Testament says that to obey is better than sacrifice (1Sa 15:22); the New Testament says: faith without works is dead (Jas 2:26).

THEY STOPPED POINTING TO THE CROSS

We learn from Scripture that the priests got **exalted above measure** to the original instructions that God established as a pattern to follow in offering of a sacrifice for sin. They stopped pointing to the cross. The priests got out of bounds of the Word. The mark of perfection that was set was not being met. The sacrifice was to be **without blemish** to be recognized as acceptable payment for sin by God. God saw what they were doing as evil. It was corruption!

> "But cursed be the deceiver, which hath in his flock a male, and voweth, and sacrificeth unto the LORD a corrupt thing: for I am a great King, saith the LORD of hosts, and my name is dreadful among the heathen." (Mal. 1:14)

By not following God's commandments and instructions, these people were about to reap the wrath of God for what they were doing. Are we as a Christian nation any different today? **Are we still pointing lost souls to the cross?** Some televangelists are not! Let us warn them. This should cause us to be more observant of God's Word.

When we read the Holy Bible, we should ask the Holy Spirit to examine our heart, for we are a nation that has been greatly blessed by the Lord. We don't sacrifice animals today because of Christ. He gave His life as payment for our sin. We've been pardoned, but where is the holiness of God? Are we following the commandments of God or just doing religious things as a ritual?

> "Examine yourselves, whether ye be in the faith; prove your own selves. Know ye not your own selves, how that Jesus Christ is in you, except ye be reprobates?" (2 Cor. 13:5)
>
> "Examine me, O LORD, and prove me; try my reins and my heart." (Ps. 26:2)

Where do we stand with what is found in the Bible? If we don't search the Scriptures, how do we know if we measure up? How do we know what pleases the Lord if our Bible is just collecting dust on a shelf?

One such case was when Hilkiah, the priest, found a book of the law by Moses from the Lord and gave it to Shaphan, the scribe, the king's press secretary. Shaphan read it to the king. It was prime time news!

"Then Shaphan the scribe told the king, saying, Hilkiah the priest hath given me a book. And Shaphan read it before the king. And it came to pass, when the king had heard the words of the law, that he rent his clothes." (2 Chron. 34:18-19)

Josiah, the king of Judah, was suddenly struck with grief and fear, after finding God's holy instructions in the Word were being ignored.

"Go, inquire of the LORD for me, and for them that are left in Israel and in Judah, concerning the words of the book that is found: for great is the wrath of the LORD that is poured out upon us, because **our fathers have not kept the word of the LORD**, to do after all that is written in this book." (2 Chron. 34:21)

WHAT WAS IN THE BOOK?

Behold! It was The Law of Moses. The news media of today would be wise to hire people like Shaphan to read The Bible to keep our nation, elected Congress and our President informed of truth.

We find that God was consulted through Huldah, the prophetess. The Lord spoke through her as such:

"Thus saith the LORD, Behold, I will bring evil upon this place, and upon the inhabitants thereof, even all the curses that are written in the book which they have read before the king of Judah:

"Because they have forsaken me, and have burned incense unto other gods, that they might provoke me to anger with all the works of their hands; therefore my wrath shall be poured out upon this place, and shall not be quenched.

"And as for the king of Judah, who sent you to inquire of the LORD, so shall ye say unto him, Thus saith the LORD God of Israel concerning the words which thou hast heard;

"Because thine heart was tender, and thou didst humble thyself before God, when thou heardest his words against this place, and against the inhabitants thereof, and humbledst thyself before me, and didst rend thy clothes, and weep before me; I have even heard thee also, saith the LORD.

"Behold, I will gather thee to thy fathers, and thou shalt be gathered to thy grave in peace, neither shall thine eyes see all the evil that I will bring upon this place, and upon the inhabitants of the same. So they brought the king word again." (2 Chron. 34:24-28)

Josiah, the king of Judah, escaped the coming judgment because he humbled himself. He feared the Lord with a tender heart and quickly changed direction to obey the Word of God.

It is possible, since we no longer sacrifice bulls, lambs and goats for our sin, that we too, have lost in the shuffle of life the values and significance of the sacrifice. Do we really understand what Jesus did for us as our sacrifice—the purpose, the reason, the fulfillment of the law, the cleansing and forgiveness of sin forever?

If our spiritual leaders were more aware of the reason for a perfect sacrifice to be without blemish, would they still have blemished views of Paul's thorn in the flesh? Perhaps the Book of Leviticus is one of modern day's most ignored books in the Bible.

BLEMISH VIEWS DO NOT LEAD TO PERFECTION

God called Paul to be an apostle of Jesus Christ; and, in his calling as an apostle, he was to write Holy Scripture, letters of the New Testament, **pointing all of mankind to the supreme sacrifice, the living sacrifice, the perfect Lamb of God, Jesus Christ.**

> "That he might present it to himself a glorious church, not having spot, or wrinkle, or any such thing; but that it should be holy and without blemish." (Eph. 5:27)

The Old Testament was a type and shadow of things to come. When we compare Old Testament Scripture of the blood sacrifice that points to the New Testament supreme sacrifice—Jesus Christ—as the point of perfection **without blemish**, as the Scripture confirms, we see that **most views** of Paul's thorn in the flesh are **giving Paul a blemish** as God's way to keep him humble.

This is a serious oversight for all who have the view that God used a blemish to keep Paul humble, as an apostle of Jesus Christ. This view would be a breach of the Word and the perfection of God. Let's consider the serious disregard of the Word by the priests:

1. They were ignoring specific sacrificial instructions given to Moses by God that point to perfection.
2. They were caught in an evil deceptive scheme.
3. God's unblemished animal sacrifice set an example of what was to come. It was a type and shadow pointing sinners to the Lamb of God, to Jesus Christ, the perfect sacrifice.

God's Word is perfect and holy, without blemish. **The call** is a perfect gift from the Lord. It pricks the flesh to live as Christ. It points to the Word—to the unblemished sacrifice—Jesus Christ. The call points back to the cross.

> "Every good gift and every perfect gift is from above, and cometh down from the Father of lights, with whom is no variableness, neither shadow of turning." (James 1:17)

David was a type of perfection without blemish. Samuel anointed David as king of Israel. From the seed of David, came Jesus Christ, unblemished, as a perfect sacrifice.

> "And he sent, and brought him in. Now he was ruddy, and withal of a beautiful countenance, and goodly to look to. And the LORD said, Arise, anoint him: for this is he." (1 Sam. 16:12)

By reviewing Bible passages of the Old Testament that reveal God's commandments and statutes in conjunction with Paul as author of Holy epistles inspired by God, it is unscriptural that God would give Paul a blemish: poor eyesight, sickness, birth defect, speech impediment, epilepsy, or disease to keep him in measure and humble.

Here are more Scriptures that invalidate and nullify all of the blemish views of Paul's thorn in the flesh:

- "For whatsoever man he be that hath a blemish, he shall not approach: a blind man, or a lame, or he that hath a flat nose, or anything superfluous, Or a man that is broken footed, or broken handed, Or crookback, or a dwarf, or that hath a blemish in his eye, or be scurvy, or scabbed, or hath his stones broken;
- "No man that hath a blemish of the seed of Aaron the priest shall come nigh to offer the

offerings of the LORD made by fire: he hath a blemish; **he shall not come nigh to offer the bread of his God.** He shall eat the bread of his God, both of the most holy, and of the holy.

- "Only he shall not go in unto the veil, nor come nigh unto the altar, because he hath a blemish; that he profane not my sanctuaries: for I the LORD do sanctify them. And Moses told it unto Aaron, and to his sons, and unto all the children of Israel." (Lev. 21:18-24)

Scripture confirms it: no one with a blemish is allowed to come unto the veil, near the altar or offer the bread of his God. **God's Word is the bread of life.** Therefore, God could not have used a defect or blemish to be the source of guidance to keep Paul humble as he wrote (the bread) and preached the Holy Word of God. The harmony and unity of Scripture always points to perfection.

Paul was not a blemish. The words Paul wrote down as God inspired them were glorious. Paul gave his life as a sacrifice unto God. The harmony of Scripture is pure and unbroken in the office of an apostle of Jesus Christ. The call was perfect and unblemished. The thorn in the flesh, the call, was perfection pointing to perfection. God used Paul to point sinners to the unblemished Lamb of God, Jesus Christ, who takes away the sins of the world.

"He is the Rock, **his work is perfect**: for all his ways are judgment: a God of truth and without iniquity, just and right is he." (Deut. 32:4)

THE THORN IN THE FLESH LEADS TO PERFECTION

1. The thorn in the flesh, **the call**, as you will discover, pointed Paul in the direction of the unblemished sacrifice, the Lamb of God, our perfect redeemer and Savior, Jesus Christ.
2. The thorn—**the call to be an apostle**—pointed Paul to live as Christ, unblemished and uncorrupted by the things of the world. His writings point all people to Jesus Christ, and he asked all who believe to follow him as he followed Christ.

<u>"The disciple is not above his master: but every one that is perfect shall be as his master." (Luke 6:40)</u>

God would not use evil in the same manner that He Himself rejects. He doesn't use the flesh to point to perfection. He uses what is perfect to point to perfection. He uses **the cross**. Authur Blessitt said, "It was at the cross where the worst of man met the best of God." Jesus on **the cross**, as a sinless perfect sacrifice, pointed to humility and love. How could God use something unacceptable or unworthy to point to humility?

> "And in process of time it came to pass, that Cain brought of the fruit of the ground an offering unto the LORD. And Abel, he also brought of the firstlings of his flock and of the fat thereof. And the LORD had respect unto Abel and to his offering: But unto Cain and to his offering he had not respect. And Cain was very wroth, and his countenance fell." (Gen. 4:3-5)

God is omniscient and knows when sin is near (Cain killed Abel his brother), and the only sacrifice that covers sin is a blood sacrifice. Cain's offering was not accepted by God because it wasn't a blood sacrifice—it didn't point to the cross—it didn't point to the Blood of Jesus Christ. It pointed to dirt, where man came from. When religion points to the works of man, it is seen as a Cain sacrifice and is not accepted by God. We know of religions in the land today that do this.

God does not use secularism, humanism or the philosophies of this world that point to dust where man is made from, in concert with the unblemished Christ, the pure Word of God. These are not a part of the restoration of fallen man. That would be unacceptable!

We must come by faith to the throne of God in sincerity and uprightness of heart, looking to Jesus as our perfect sacrifice. Only then, will we have assurance of forgiveness of sin. His Blood paid in full the debt we owed because of our sin.

When Jesus intercedes on our behalf, our Petitioner has no stain of sin. His Blood makes us perfect. The life of Christ that was in the Blood was sacrificed for us. God looks through the Blood that sanctifies and hides our sinful past. His Blood covers all our wasted years, lived in acts of sin. He makes us into a new creation. We are cleansed, sanctified and made holy through the body of Jesus Christ.

> "In burnt offerings and sacrifices for sin thou hast had no pleasure. Then said I, Lo, I come (in the volume of the book it is written of me,) to do thy will, O God. Above when he said, Sacrifice and offering and burnt offerings and offering for sin thou wouldest not, neither hadst pleasure therein; which are offered by the law; Then said he, Lo, I come to do thy will, O God. He taketh away the first, that he may establish the second. By the which will we are sanctified through the offering of the body of Jesus Christ once for all." (Heb. 10:6-10)

By searching for truth in the spirit realm of perfection that controls the sin nature (flesh), and not looking for truth in the physical nature of the flesh, we find the answer. The thorn in the flesh pricked the conscious flesh—the sin nature, and had nothing to do with the physical flesh. The physical body of Paul didn't know there was a thorn.

If you lift ten pounds of honey, it's done by the physical strength within you. If you say something immoral to someone, it's from the sin nature (flesh) that you say it. The physical flesh is not under condemnation of the law by what was done from the carnal flesh. However, the physical flesh may tremble when the brain's alarm signal sends the nervous system a message of grave danger or a future penalty.

The call to be an apostle of Jesus Christ was the perfect guidance system that kept Paul in character to the Word for the epistles he was to pen. The call pointed to the Word. That's why the call to be an apostle of Jesus Christ was the thorn in the flesh. It's the Word!

Only God could create such a brilliant guidance system to control the behavior of man. It covers all the essentials of current life, as well as eternal life. It points to the holiness of Christ. It points to the **law of the Spirit of life in Christ.** How could there be something better? You'll be amazed when you learn more about it.

"And what nation is there so great, that hath statutes and judgments so righteous as all this law, which I set before you this day? Only take heed to thyself, and keep thy soul diligently, lest thou forget the things which thine eyes have seen, and lest they depart from thy heart all the days of thy life: but teach them thy sons, and thy sons' sons;

"Specially the day that thou stoodest before the LORD thy God in Horeb, when the LORD said unto me, Gather me the people together, and I will make them hear my words, that they may learn to fear me all the days that they shall live upon the earth, and that they may teach their children." (Deut. 4:8-10)

Ignoring God's commandments, statutes and judgments causes unnecessary pain and suffering. Some recognize their sin and quickly repent; but all too often, people live the way of the world and don't search to know God. It happens to all who fail to come to **the saving knowledge of Jesus Christ** or take the Word of God seriously.

"Let thine ear now be attentive, and thine eyes open, that thou mayest hear the prayer of thy servant, which I pray before thee now, day and night, for the children of Israel thy servants, and confess the sins of the children of Israel, which we have sinned against thee: both I and my father's house have sinned. We have dealt very corruptly against thee, and have not kept the commandments, nor the statutes, nor the judgments, which thou commandedst thy servant Moses." (Neh. 1:6-7)

Today, some spiritual leaders make similar mistakes due to a failure of fully comprehending the sacrifice that Christ made. The purpose and reason for the unblemished sacrifice is in God's character.

What does the Word say? "For as often as ye eat this bread, and drink this cup, ye do shew the Lord's death till he come. Wherefore whosoever shall eat this bread, and drink this cup of the Lord, unworthily, shall be guilty of the body and blood of the Lord. But let a man examine himself, and so let him eat of that bread, and drink of that cup. For he that eateth and drinketh unworthily, eateth and drinketh damnation to himself, **not discerning the Lord's body**. For this cause many are **weak and sickly among you, and many sleep**." (1 Cor. 11:26-30)

There are two major issues here to address. One is the heart issue, which is always personal between God and the one taking communion. It is entering into a sacred moment of meditation on the Lord in remembering His sinless (unblemished) life and death on the cross. It is a sacred time of self-examination, looking introspectively at our person, behavior, character and relationship with Christ.

The other issue is that we properly discern the Lord's body. His body and blood is the New Testament. We are to eat and drink Christ. It is the Lord's Last Will and Testament for our inheritance. By fully discerning His body, the New Testament, we put our own life into **spiritual action with His resurrected life**. Moreover, it positions us to avoid weakness, sickness or an untimely death. Regarding the Will, many who are entitled to a large share of the richest estate ever willed to a person, don't realize that it will be given to another without their soon claim. Many have never read **the Will** to receive their inheritance. The believer must activate the Will by being fully engaged by faith in the victory walk of the cross. The **law of the Spirit of life in Christ** is what guarantees our victory over all sin.

THE KINGDOM OF HEAVEN IS LIKE:

"And I was afraid, and went and hid thy talent in the earth: lo, there thou hast that is thine. His lord answered and said unto him, Thou wicked and slothful servant, thou knewest that I reap where I sowed not, and gather where I have not strawed: Thou oughtest therefore to have put my money to the exchangers, and then at my coming I should have received mine own with usury. Take therefore the talent from him, and give it unto him which hath ten talents." (Matt. 25:25-28)

Early in church history, the Corinthians were instructed by Paul to live in sincerity and truth. He warned them of the **dangers of leaven** and gave them a pure and sure foundation in the glorious Gospel.

> "Your glorying is not good. Know ye not that a little leaven leaveneth the whole lump? Purge out therefore the old leaven, that ye may be a new lump, as ye are unleavened. For even Christ our Passover is sacrificed for us: **Therefore let us keep the feast, not with old leaven**, neither with the leaven of malice and wickedness; **but with the unleavened bread** of sincerity and truth." (1 Cor. 5:6-8)

This is the very reason we are to take of the Lord's Supper often. Each time we take of the Lord's Supper, we re-examine current personal issues in life by the body and blood of Christ. It is a spiritual check-up to see if we are still living by the New Testament, the Lord's last Will of Victory in the cross.

> Jesus set the example. "And he that sent me is with me: the Father hath not left me alone; for I do always those things that please him." (John 8:29)

When we please God, it is our guarantee that nothing is withheld from us by God's displeasure. Also, the Lord is more readily available to our needs when we work to correct our faults and ask forgiveness of others. The psalmist wrote an example of this:

> "Search me, O God, and know my heart: try me, and know my thoughts: And see if there be any wicked way in me, and lead me in the way everlasting." (Ps. 139:23-24)

When we are in obedience with God's Word, we find spiritual favor and He showers us with spiritual comfort, peace and blessings.

If the sacrifice was not perfect, God would not have accepted the sacrifice as payment for sin. The sacrifice would not have fulfilled the law. By Jesus Christ being perfect, without sin, and dying on the cross, He became God's accepted payment for sin. Thank the Lord for His death and sacrifice on the cross.

We are forever indebted to Jesus Christ, as our Redeemer. He became the author and finisher of our faith.

> "Wherefore seeing we also are compassed about with so great a cloud of witnesses, let us lay aside every weight, and the sin which doth so easily beset us, and let us run with patience the race that is set before us, Looking unto Jesus the author and finisher of our faith; who for the joy that was set before him endured

the cross, despising the shame, and is set down at the right hand of the throne of God." (Heb. 12:1-2)

When we understand why the sacrifice had to be perfect and its depth more completely, it astounds us to learn some of the significant benefits that are ours by what Jesus did for us by being perfect.

WHO IS WORTHY TO OPEN THE BOOK?

"And I saw in the right hand of him that sat on the throne a book written within and on the backside, sealed with seven seals. And I saw a strong angel proclaiming with a loud voice, Who is worthy to open the book, and to loose the seals thereof? And no man in heaven, nor in earth, neither under the earth, was able to open the book, neither to look thereon. And I wept much, because no man was found worthy to open and to read the book, neither to look thereon." (Rev 5:1-4)

Let us consider some of our heroes of faith:

- Enoch walked with God and was no more, for God took him.
- Abraham was our father of faith.

- Joseph had dreams from God.
- Moses, the man God spoke face to face as a man speaks unto his friend.
- David had a heart for God.
- Mary, the mother of Jesus.

None of these heroes of our faith were worthy to open the book. Who then is worthy?

> "And one of the elders saith unto me, Weep not: behold, the Lion of the tribe of Judah, the Root of David, hath prevailed to open the book, and to loose the seven seals thereof. And I beheld, and, lo, in the midst of the throne and of the four beasts, and in the midst of the elders, stood a Lamb as it had been slain, having seven horns and seven eyes, which are the seven Spirits of God sent forth into all the earth." (Rev 5:5-6)

When we attend church, we do so to give our redeemer praise, honor and glory. When we pray, we come boldly **through the blood** of Jesus to make our request, known to God. All whose lives have been redeemed know that He alone, and no other, is worthy of our spiritual songs, worship and praise.

"And when he had taken the book, the four beasts and four and twenty elders fell down before the Lamb, having every one of them **harps**, and golden vials full of odours, which are the **prayers of saints**. And they sung a **new song**, saying, Thou art worthy to take the book, and to open the seals thereof: for thou wast slain, and hast redeemed us to God by thy blood out of every kindred, and tongue, and people, and nation; And hast made us unto our God kings and priests: and we shall reign on the earth." (Rev 5:8-10)

Here is what the perfect sacrifice reveals:

1. The law can only be fulfilled by a perfect sacrifice.
2. It takes perfection to redeem sinners.
3. It brings true interpretation to the Scriptures.
4. It reveals the character of God.
5. It exposes false religions and teachings (being mislead).
6. It reveals who the mediator between God and man is.
7. It is the only accepted payment for the debt of sin.
8. It provides everlasting life and eternal security to the believer.
9. It defeats and disarms the enemy.
10. It removes the guilt of sin.

11. It reveals how marvelous and great the love of God is for you and me.
12. It speaks of perfection, holiness and righteousness.
13. It brings faith, hope and love to the believer.
14. It speaks of amazing grace.
15. It reveals that the cross of Christ alone is the victory over sin.
16. It gives birth to songs of victory in Christ.
17. His perfect sacrifice made Him the only one worthy to open the book.
18. It brings **worship of Jesus Christ** and Him alone into the House of God.

If the sacrifice was blemished, it would stain **the testimony brought before the witnesses**. It would mar the evidence of **Scripture**. It would not surpass the **Mosaic Law**.

Fifty days after Jesus, our Passover Lamb, was crucified, the Holy Ghost came and filled the whole house where the disciples were sitting. He gave the Lord's disciples **power to witness** to all people about the Resurrected Christ who paid the debt of sin and restored everlasting fellowship with a Holy God.

> "But **ye shall receive power**, after that the Holy Ghost is come upon you: and ye shall be witnesses unto me both in Jerusalem, and in all Judaea, and in

Samaria, and unto the uttermost part of the earth." (Acts 1:8)

The Holy Spirit could not abide within the hearts of Old Testament believers because the sin debt had not yet been paid. Up until the time of the Passover, the law was our schoolmaster; but when Jesus gave himself as the perfect sacrifice, we were no longer under the law, but under grace through faith in Christ.

"But the Scripture hath concluded all under sin, that the promise by faith of Jesus Christ might be given to them that believe. But before faith came, we were kept under the law, shut up unto the faith which should afterwards be revealed.

"Wherefore the law was our schoolmaster to bring us unto Christ, that we might be justified by faith. But after that faith is come, we are no longer under a schoolmaster. For ye are all the children of God by faith in Christ Jesus." (Gal. 3:22-26)

At Pentecost, which was predicted in the Book of Leviticus, the Holy Ghost gave believers power for anointed service. He also came to reprove the world of sin, and of righteousness and of judgment.

"And ye shall count unto you from the morrow after the sabbath, from the day that ye brought the sheaf of the wave offering; seven sabbaths shall be complete: Even unto the morrow after the seventh sabbath shall ye number fifty days; and ye shall offer a new meat offering unto the LORD." (Lev. 23:15-16)

After Pentecost came, Peter made **gospel headlines** in Jerusalem when confronted by the high priest for witnessing and speaking out about the Lord. He boldly proclaimed man's supreme authority and the way of salvation:

"Then Peter and the other apostles answered and said, We ought to obey God rather than men. The God of our fathers raised up Jesus, whom ye slew and hanged on a tree. Him hath God exalted with his right hand to be a Prince and a Saviour, for to give repentance to Israel, and forgiveness of sins.

"And we are his witnesses of these things; and so is also the Holy Ghost, **whom God hath given to them that obey him**. When they heard that, they were cut to the heart, and took counsel to slay them." (Acts 5:29-33)

Dr. Gamaliel, a law professor, stepped forward to defend the apostles. Scripture shows that Paul, as a young man, was working on a law degree, because he sat at the feet of law professor Dr. Gamaliel in the city of Jerusalem.

> "Then stood there up one in the council, a Pharisee, named Gamaliel, a doctor of the law, had in reputation among all the people, and commanded to put the apostles forth a little space; And said unto them, Ye men of Israel, take heed to yourselves what ye intend to do as touching these men." (Acts 5:34-35)
>
> "I am verily a man which am a Jew, born in Tarsus, a city in Cilicia, yet brought up in this city at the feet of Gamaliel, and taught according to the perfect manner of the law of the fathers, and was zealous toward God, as ye all are this day." (Acts 22:3)

In Acts, chapter nine, when Paul (Saul) was on the road to Damascus, he may have been on assignment from the city council that Dr. Gamaliel evidently was a member of, when he was enforcing the Law of Moses and seeking to destroy those not following the commandments of God. The law he falsely assumed was being broken by some of the disciples of Jesus, is found in Deuteronomy:

> "If thy brother, the son of thy mother, or thy son, or thy daughter, or the wife of thy bosom, or thy friend, which is as thine own soul, entice thee

secretly, saying, Let us go and serve other gods, which thou hast not known, thou, nor thy fathers;" (Deut. 13:6)

"But thou shalt surely kill him; thine hand shall be first upon him to put him to death, and afterwards the hand of all the people. And thou shalt stone him with stones, that he die; because he hath sought to thrust thee away from the Lord thy God, which brought thee out of the land of Egypt, from the house of bondage." (Deut. 13:9-10)

Some religious Jews were ignorant of the fact and truth that this Jesus the disciples were serving was the same God, Yahweh, the Lord, and Elohiym, God of Abraham and Moses. They just didn't have up-to-date knowledge of the Word of God. They were not in tune with the Holy Ghost in what God was doing concerning the law.

"For the law having a shadow of good things to come, and not the very image of the things, can never with those sacrifices which they offered year by year continually make the comers thereunto perfect." (Heb. 10:1)

The Holy Ghost came with convicting power, bringing sinners to repentance and a saving knowledge of Jesus Christ through the cross. This mighty move of God came to Jerusalem and brought high definition to the past, present and future—the past is trying to keep the law (which no one can)—the present is being saved by grace through faith in Christ—and on to the future, following the dictates of the Holy Spirit as we walk in the **law of the Spirit of life in Christ** and not in the flesh.

> "Now we have received, not the spirit of the world, but the spirit which is of God; that we might know the things that are freely given to us of God. Which things also we speak, not in the words which man's wisdom teacheth, but which the Holy Ghost teacheth; comparing spiritual things with spiritual." (1 Cor. 2:12-13)

The finger of God first engraved the law upon stone; but with the advent of the Holy Spirit, God engraves the Word upon the fleshy tablets of our heart. It is a "change of guard" over our life. The Spirit of God, which is more glorious than the law, makes us ministers of the spirit in righteousness by grace through faith.

> "Forasmuch as ye are manifestly declared to be the epistle of Christ ministered by us, written not with ink, but with the Spirit of the living God; not in tables of stone, but in fleshy tables of the heart. And such trust have we through Christ to God-ward:

"Not that we are sufficient of ourselves to think anything as of ourselves; but our sufficiency is of God; Who also hath made us able ministers of the new testament; not of the letter, but of the spirit: for the letter killeth, but the spirit giveth life.

"But if the ministration of death, written and engraven in stones, was glorious, so that the children of Israel could not stedfastly behold the face of Moses for the glory of his countenance; which glory was to be done away:

"How shall not the ministration of the spirit be rather glorious? For if the ministration of condemnation be glory, much more doth the ministration of righteousness exceed in glory.

"For even that which was made glorious had no glory in this respect, by reason of the glory that excelleth. For if that which is done away was glorious, much more that which remaineth is glorious." (2 Cor. 3:3-11)

Indeed, we have become the epistle of Christ through His life-giving Spirit. Our lives show Jesus to the unbelieving world. Oh what a joy to know Him. An example of the Spirit having supreme authority over the law is when the Holy Ghost empowered Stephen to speak words of conviction. It caused a mighty uproar with Jews, who were not keeping the law, and who were unyielding to the Holy Ghost. Stephen's speech offended them greatly:

> "Ye stiffnecked and uncircumcised in heart and ears, ye do always resist the Holy Ghost: as your fathers did, so do ye. Which of the prophets have not your father's persecuted? and they have slain them which shewed before of the coming of the Just One; of whom ye have been now the betrayers and murderers: Who have received the law by the disposition of angels, and have not kept it. When they heard these things, they were cut to the heart, and they gnashed on him with their teeth." (Acts 7:51-54)

The Jews were confronted by the Holy Ghost through Stephen. Saul was there watching. It was around this time that Saul may have signed up for a religious mission: to search for any who belonged to this Way and bring them bound to Jerusalem. We find him on the way to Damascus in command of a **religion-of-law** war party.

SAUL'S CONVERSION

"And Saul, yet breathing out threatenings and slaughter against the disciples of the Lord, went unto the high priest, And desired of him letters to Damascus to the synagogues, that if he found any of this way, whether they were men or women, he might bring them bound unto Jerusalem.

"And as he journeyed, he came near Damascus: and suddenly there shined round about him a light from heaven: And he fell to the earth, and heard a voice saying unto him, Saul, Saul, why persecutest thou me?

"And he said, Who art thou, Lord? And the Lord said, I am Jesus whom thou persecutest: it is hard for thee to kick against the pricks. And he trembling and astonished said, Lord, what wilt thou have me to do? And the Lord said unto him, Arise, and go into the city, and it shall be told thee what thou must do. And the men which journeyed with him stood speechless, hearing a voice, but seeing no man.

"And Saul arose from the earth; and when his eyes were opened, he saw no man: but they led him by the hand, and brought him into Damascus. And he was three days without sight, and neither did eat nor drink." (Acts 9:1-9)

Glory! His spiritual eyes were opened to understand who Jesus Christ is. Meeting Jesus face-to-face canceled the religious plan he had. When Paul called out, "Who art thou Lord?" he instantly changed from being religious to having a personal relationship with the risen Lord.

Jesus responded, "I am Jesus whom thou persecutest."

Those words brought the light to Paul to understand the Gospel, **the Way**. He suddenly realized he had been the enemy of God taking prisoner those He loved, who followed this new way—what a shock!

It was the old covenant resistance of the **new covenant**. Paul (Saul) was wholly in allegiance to the old—the laws of Moses. He had believed that the disciples of this Jesus (**of this way**) were serving another god.

Thus, he was persecuting **those of the Way**, the new covenant, the New Testament church. The Old Testament was fulfilled by the death, burial and resurrection of Jesus Christ. Also, he was kicking against Peter, James and John who were pillars of the New Testament church.

Many of the Jews living in the Promised Land were just not up on Scripture knowledge and current events. Did they fail to take Jesus' advice concerning the doctrine of the Pharisees and of the Sadducees?

> "For the Sadducees say that there is no resurrection, neither angel, nor spirit: but the Pharisees confess both." (Acts 23:8)

Indeed, the mindset of many Jews was that they were looking for a king to set up his throne over the land of Israel. Sadly, even today, many of the Jews are still looking for their Messiah to show up. Only recognizing the Old Testament, they reject Jesus as their Messiah.

Let's take a moment to reflect upon our faith and knowledge of the Word. Do we really know Him? Many that attend church do so because of tradition and religion and have no personal relationship with the living Christ. These people may not make it to heaven! I've talked to pastors about this, and they're concerned. These people attend meetings, but never bring the fruit of faith to the church.

Even the Lord's disciples were caught up in the Laws of Moses; they were persistent to enforce the law of circumcision. Most Jews felt justified by the Law. Paul began preaching salvation by grace through faith in Christ as the way, and not by works of the law.

FINDING THE SECRET BEHIND PAUL'S THORN

To find the place where the thorn in the flesh made itself known to Paul, we need to retrace the beginning of his ministry. What happened from the Damascus road experience to Damascus, then to Arabia, back to Damascus, and then at Jerusalem? This will take some spiritual detective work to uncover the mystery. What did Jesus say to Paul? What can we establish as fact and truth? What evidence is there from the witnesses: Peter, James, John, Barnabas, Ananias and others?

> "And there was a certain disciple at Damascus, named Ananias; and to him said the Lord in a vision, Ananias. And he said, Behold, I am here, Lord. And the Lord said unto him, Arise, and go into the street which is called Straight, and inquire in the house of Judas for one called Saul, of Tarsus: for, behold,

he prayeth, And hath seen in a vision a man named Ananias coming in, and putting his hand on him, that he might receive his sight.

"Then Ananias answered, Lord, I have heard by many of this man, how much evil he hath done to thy saints at Jerusalem: And here he hath authority from the chief priests to bind all that call on thy name. **But the Lord said unto him, Go thy way: for he is a chosen vessel unto me, to bear my name before the Gentiles, and kings, and the children of Israel:** For I will shew him how great things he must suffer for my name's sake.

"And Ananias went his way, and entered into the house; and putting his hands on him said, Brother Saul, the Lord, even Jesus, that appeared unto thee in the way as thou camest, hath sent me, that thou mightest receive thy sight, **and be filled with the Holy Ghost**.

"And immediately there fell from his eyes as it had been scales: and he received sight forthwith, and arose, and was baptized. And when he had received meat, he was strengthened. Then was Saul certain days with the disciples which were at Damascus." (Acts 9:10-19)

In our search, the thorn in the flesh must match the DNA of the Gospel. If we recreate the scene, what caused Paul to describe a hurt or pain as a thorn in the flesh? Was the pain from words he had spoken, some wrongful act he did or was it physical pain?

The secret cannot be discovered without getting inside the ministry of the Gospel with Paul and walking the spiritual walk of his journeys. To search out the deep things of God, we must walk in the Word with the Spirit of God.

> "But God hath revealed them unto us by his Spirit: for the Spirit searcheth all things, yea, the deep things of God." (1 Cor. 2:11)

The thorn in the flesh has many pieces to connect (like a puzzle) before it can be fully understood. The pieces fit together to distinguish an apostle of Jesus Christ, revealing: purpose, guidance, position, motivation, boundary and destination. All this is found in the Word.

> "But if our gospel be hid, it is hid to them that are lost: In whom the god of this world hath blinded the minds of them which believe not, lest the light of the glorious gospel of Christ, who is the image of God, should shine unto them." (2 Cor. 4:3-4)

It all started with the flesh-light knock-down experience on the Damascus road. It will be very interesting to find out how Paul's conversion and calling was received by the church, the disciples and the apostles. Let's examine their response to the man that once persecuted the Church. Were they excited when they learned that Paul was equally ranked as an apostle of Jesus Christ?

Did they have Paul sit between Peter and James on the podium while John announced the good news to the Church? Who were the ones that had the quick-draw to forgive Paul of his past sins of persecuting the Church? Were there signs of resentment from other leaders? Was there joy unspeakable and agape love when he came to meet them?

To answer these questions, we must go to the Scripture account of that meeting with the leaders of the church and let it reveal the truth as to what the thorn in the flesh was—when it happened, why it happened and its purpose; then identify some of the saints that were there on location that glorious day of the Lord.

> "But I certify you, brethren, that the gospel which was preached of me is not after man. For I neither received it of man, neither was I taught it, but by the revelation of Jesus Christ. For ye have heard of my conversation in time past in the Jews' religion, how that beyond measure I persecuted the church of God, and wasted it: And profited in the Jews' religion above many my equals in mine own nation, being more exceedingly zealous of the traditions of my fathers.

"But when it pleased God, who separated me from my mother's womb, and called me by his grace, To reveal his Son in me, that I might preach him among the heathen; immediately I conferred not with flesh and blood: Neither went I up to Jerusalem to them which were apostles before me; but I went into Arabia, and returned again unto Damascus." (Gal. 1:11-17)

The Gospel wasn't man's gospel, taught by man; but it came by revelation of Jesus Christ. How interesting to study the change in Paul, who once knew only the law, the Jews' religion.

"For when Moses had spoken every precept to all the people according to the law, he took the blood of calves and of goats, with water, and scarlet wool, and hyssop, and sprinkled both the book, and all the people," (Heb. 9:19)

This was all done before the birth, death, burial and resurrection of Jesus Christ. Jesus became the Lamb that was slain for payment of sin; therefore, we no longer need to make sacrifices. The Old Testament was fulfilled by the coming of Jesus Christ. The old order was fulfilled and a new order began. The new order was the New Covenant, the New Testament, or the testimony of Jesus Christ.

"And for this cause he is the mediator of the New Testament, that by means of death, for the redemption of the transgressions that were under the first testament, they which are called might receive the promise of eternal inheritance." (Heb. 9:15)

Paul met the mediator between God and man on the road to Damascus—the resurrected Christ—and His call would give birth to the divinely-inspired Word. When he told about the visions and revelations he had had, he was in Christ and Christ was in him. Being in Christ is walking in the Word, for Jesus is the Word. Paul willingly became a prisoner of the Lord Jesus Christ. He gave the key to his heart to Jesus and lived for Him only.

VISIONS AND REVELATIONS

We know that Arabia is most likely the place where Paul received visions and revelations, because he said they came to him **above fourteen years ago.** It would place Paul in Arabia when the Lord took him to paradise. He spent quality time with the Lord in Arabia, receiving divine supernatural instructions for special service.

> "It is not expedient for me doubtless to glory. I will come to visions and revelations of the Lord. I knew a man **in Christ** above fourteen years ago, (whether in the body, I cannot tell; or whether out of the body, I cannot tell: God knoweth;) such an one caught up to the third heaven.
>
> "And I knew such a man, (whether in the body, or out of the body, I cannot tell: God knoweth;) How that he was caught up into paradise, and heard unspeakable words, which it is not lawful for a man to utter." (2 Cor. 12:1-4)

Paul is talking about himself when he says, "I knew a man **in Christ** above fourteen years ago." It is through these visions and revelations that he was called to be an apostle of the Lord Jesus Christ. His initial call came to him on the Damascus road; but the call to be an apostle of Jesus Christ most likely came while in Arabia after being filled with the Holy Ghost in Damascus.

When he went back to Damascus from Arabia, his spiritual goals were set for eternity. I believe he got a glimpse of unworthy sinners like me coming to the cross for salvation through his epistles. He saw your destiny and mine with the Lord, and it ignited an eternal flame.

He confounded the Jews that lived in Damascus, proving that this is the very Christ. In Damascus, Saul (Paul) made Satan furious by preaching the Gospel, because some of the Jews wanted to kill him.

> "But Saul increased the more in strength, and confounded the Jews which dwelt at Damascus, proving that this is very Christ. And after that many days were fulfilled, the Jews took counsel to kill him: But their laying await was known of Saul. And they watched the gates day and night to kill him. Then the disciples took him by night, and let him down by the wall in a basket." (Acts 9:22-25)

After being let down the wall in a basket, Paul headed off to Jerusalem to see the apostles. He was excited to tell the Lord's disciples of his experience with Jesus and let the other apostles know that God had moved him from the status of an ordinary Jewish citizen, who was zealous for the laws of Moses and obedience to God's law, to the high rank of an apostle.

> "Then **after three years** I went up to Jerusalem to see Peter, and abode with him fifteen days. But other of the apostles saw I none, save James the Lord's brother. Now the things which I write unto you, behold, before God, I lie not." (Gal. 1:18-20)

He had met the God of an everlasting kingdom. Now he was about to meet some of the servants of the King's Son. On the way to Jerusalem, he could not get the visions and revelations off his mind. He had been caught up into the third heaven. It revealed God's purpose for his future. Now, at last, that day had arrived.

He is thinking about the office of the apostleship and how he would conduct such a high office. He is thrilled to join the team. He believes he is a sure thing for the high office. He is God's choice for the office. He knows that he has higher credentials than his fellow Jews concerning the traditions of Abraham, Isaac, Jacob and the laws of Moses.

"And profited in the Jews' religion above many my equals in mine own nation, being more exceedingly zealous of the traditions of my fathers." (Gal. 1:14)

The past and the future were on his mind. Paul fully realized the great commission that Christ had anointed him to fulfill. He knew many Jews were completely misinformed and were living in the same conflict to the truth that he once had.

Many of the Jews were not aware that God had just fulfilled the greatest prophecy ever—and it had happened on their watch. Some blindly took part in the crucifixion. Others were too busy talking about and enforcing the Laws of Moses, particularly circumcision, and were totally unaware who Jesus Christ was. Very few knew that the Old Testament was complete and the law fulfilled by the death, burial and resurrection of Christ. Their only justification for sin was trying to adhere to the Laws of Moses.

"Be it known unto you therefore, men and brethren, that through this man is preached unto you the forgiveness of sins: And by him all that believe are justified from all things, from which ye could not be justified by the Law of Moses." (Acts 13:38-39)

The stage was set for the appointed high-level meeting in Jerusalem. Paul may have fasted for many hours or days.

He was ready to start new churches throughout all of Israel. He would appoint pastors and teachers for the perfecting of the saints—for the work of the ministry—for the edifying of the body of Christ.

Paul was ready to meet the apostles of the Lord Jesus Christ and to take full command of the office of an apostle. The secret behind Paul's thorn in the flesh is about to be made known.

REJECTED AS AN APOSTLE

"And when Saul was come to Jerusalem, he assayed to join himself to the disciples: but they were all afraid of him, and believed not that he was a disciple." (Acts 9:26)

Whoa! What kind of a reception was this for the one who later became the author of thirteen or fourteen (Hebrews) books of the Bible? He was not accepted as an apostle by the disciples in Jerusalem. He was devastated by their rejection. It was like making a re-entry from outer space. The re-entry burn scorched his brain and left a vapor trail of his ego. It still casts an invisible shadow to this day from the eastern sky over a narrow road that leads out of Jerusalem to Tarsus. He was weakened by the bad news. It took his breath away. It sapped his strength. He went numb.

The rejection by the disciples was a shockwave to his **ego**. God called him to be an apostle of Jesus Christ, but God had failed to tell the other apostles that He had called Paul to join them. Why didn't God send an angel like Gabriel to make an advance announcement of the apostleship of Paul to the other disciples like He did with Zacharias, father of John the Baptist, or Mary, the mother of the Jesus?

Why wasn't he warned? It was a sonic boom to his ego! It rattled him. He had never experienced such a setback. This was traumatic to his soul. **It humbled him!**

Suddenly, the truth hit him—he had spoken too soon. **He had told some followers of Christ that he was an apostle of Jesus Christ.** He did it because the visions and revelations had taken him far out into the future where all saints, apostles and disciples knew him as: Paul an apostle of Jesus Christ. He was speaking as though he was in the future—but he was in the now—he was in real time and not in future time.

We don't know the exact spot where he first told some followers of Christ that he was an apostle of Jesus Christ. It may have been on the way to Damascus from Arabia, or maybe he said it while he was in Damascus. It's possible it happened on the way to Jerusalem. What is important to know is the announcement that he was an apostle of Jesus Christ was spoken before he ever met the apostles.

You and I know Paul as an apostle of Jesus Christ because of **Bible history**. We look back on Bible history, but Paul was looking ahead at his position in the **law of the Spirit of life in Christ** that would become Bible history. He was still caught up in the moment and spoke, knowing the future, but being in real time—in the now. He may have seen a picture of you and me reading his epistles. God may have shown him a picture in the future of you and me in a Bible study discussing the wonderful truth of God's Word. When he was caught up into the third heaven, it was like a time-capsule revelation of how God was going to use him and what was going to come to pass in the future.

He was so caught up into what God had revealed in the visions and revelations, that while the message of the vision was still hot and aflame in his heart, he told a group of followers of Christ that he was an apostle of Jesus Christ. It happened before he got to Jerusalem.

He was absolutely sure that as soon as he arrived in Jerusalem he would be accepted as an apostle. God had called him into the apostleship, but to seal the apostleship, he first must report to the other apostles. He began to visualize that glorious moment of telling them of his conversion on the road to Damascus, of Ananias healing his blinded eyes, and the call—the apostleship. And oh yes, what about what Jesus told Ananias? The words of Jesus Christ are as good as gold—you can take it to the bank. Jesus is the one that set this up in the beginning, and so it has got to happen.

> "But the Lord said unto him, Go thy way: for he is a chosen vessel unto me, to bear my name before the

> Gentiles, and kings, and the children of Israel:" (Acts 9:15)

His mind had been in a state of ecstasy ever since being caught up to the third heaven, and now his heart was burning to share the good news with the other apostles. He was walking tall. He was pumped up. He could hardly contain himself. At this point he may have been in a slight state of egotism.

Fact is, and truth is, he **was** a chosen vessel of the Lord. The Lord had called Paul to be an apostle of Jesus Christ. Most of his epistles are addressed as Paul, an apostle of Jesus Christ.

> "**Paul, an apostle of Jesus Christ** by the commandment of God our Saviour, and Lord Jesus Christ, which is our hope;" (1 Tim. 1:1)

REJECTION MAKES A WEB OF FAITH INSIDE THE SECRET

Then wham—**"Rejected As An Apostle"** blazed across Paul's conscious mind! What a shock! The flesh knew something big had gone wrong, and the flesh was the guilty party. Rejection lit up Paul's flesh, and it was grandstanding with flashing distress signals. **The thorn in the flesh made its grand entry**, <u>piercing even to the dividing asunder of soul and spirit, and of the joints and marrow.</u>

The rejection by the disciples enlightened Paul's spiritual eyes to how weak the flesh is. He felt betrayed! He had felt great the day before. It was exciting to be alive and nothing bothered Paul's flesh. Fact is, he had soared with delight. But all in one moment, he discovered how weak the flesh is. It cannot discern the future in spiritual things—only the Spirit knows the future by the word of wisdom. The Spirit is not the one guilty of weakness or condemnation.

"There is therefore now no condemnation to them which are in Christ Jesus, who walk not after the flesh, but after the Spirit." (Rom. 8:1)

Paul now began to understand the difference between the flesh speaking and the Spirit of God speaking through him. He had been so excited about the good news from God and the experience of paradise that he spoke too soon.

His flesh **spoke in weakness** that he was an apostle before the appointed time of being received (approved) as an apostle by the pillars of the church—Peter, James and John. No one knew what he felt and what the rejection did. It was his secret!

MOSES HAD SOMETHING LIKE PAUL'S THORN

God planned for Moses to lead the children of Israel out of bondage. Moses knew he was the one to do it; and when he thought it was time to start the process, he was rejected and had to wait forty more years before he stretched his hand out over the sea.

"For he supposed his brethren would have understood how that God by his hand would deliver them: but they understood not." (Acts 7:25)

Why didn't the apostles believe that Paul was one of them? Didn't they see God's transforming power working in him? He had the smile, the joy and the song, 'Oh victory in Jesus.' He carried no burden of sin—the Blood of Christ had washed it all away. He had no sorrow or grief. He had the love of Jesus all over him. He had been changed! He had a new heart, a new talk and a new walk. What more evidence would they want?

Yet, the pillars of the church only knew Saul (Paul) as a persecutor of Christians. When he was a young man, witnesses laid their clothes at his feet the day Stephen was stoned. It also may have irked some disciples of the Lord, hearing that he had the high rank of an apostle.

> "As for Saul, he made havock of the church, entering into every house, and haling men and women committed them to prison." (Acts 8:3)

Sadly, there is still resentment in the church today. Like Jonah did, some take exception to the fact that redeemed sinners are getting off without paying a stiff price. How could God forgive him so quickly for what he's done? Why not at least make the sinner sweat it out for awhile?

> "And God saw their works, that they turned from their evil way; and God repented of the evil, that he

had said that he would do unto them; and he did it not." (Jonah 3:10)

"But it displeased Jonah exceedingly, and he was very angry." (Jonah 4:1)

God responds to Jonah:

"And should not I spare Nineveh, that great city, wherein are more than sixscore thousand persons that cannot discern between their right hand and their left hand; and also much cattle?" (Jonah 4:11)

God is full of compassion and mercy, and loves to see the sinner turn from sin to trust in the Lord. The Lord has the quick-draw to forgive, to pardon and to set the captive free. God wants to give us a position of value in the good—news life. But on the other side of the spectrum, Satan is so full of hate that he goes to the extreme to promote the bad. Satan gives bad news free space on prime-time.

It seems that bad news travels faster than good news. It breaks all laws—doesn't stop for little old ladies, school-crossings, signal lights or stop signs. It has no mercy or grace. Satan most likely heard about Paul's rejection through the church gossip channel. He must have been too far away to appear himself. Or we could predict that Satan, too proud, too self-important, too self-indulged to appear himself, sent a stunning message to Saul by way of a messenger.

Did Satan's messenger ask, "Saul, do you believe the Father, the Son and the Holy Spirit agree as one concerning the Gospel?"

> "For there are three that bear record in heaven, the Father, the Word, and the Holy Ghost: and these three are one." (1 John 5:7)

Saul: "Yes I do!"

The messenger then may have asked, "Do you believe that Peter, James and John agree with God as one about the preaching and teaching of the Gospel?"

Saul: "Yes, I absolutely do!"

Satan's messenger then may have buffeted Saul with words like, "Well, Peter, James and John don't agree with you that you're an apostle. If you were an apostle, they would know that you are one; but you don't have any credentials to prove that you're an apostle of Jesus Christ. You are a liar—a false prophet." Then, wouldn't you know it, the messenger reminded Saul that his character is now ruined and any future words he might speak for the Gospel will only fall on deaf ears, unheeded, to the ground.

Rejection by the church was the beginning of knowledge that there was a thorn in the flesh. Paul was devastated! He thought about the day he was called by God to be an apostle of Jesus Christ. Why hadn't the Lord told Peter,

James and John—the pillars of the church—that He had called him to be an apostle of Jesus Christ?

If only he had waited until the apostles had recognized him as an apostle, this would not have been a thorn in the flesh. Now it was too late, for he had already spoken that he was an apostle. He knew that ego, which belongs to the family of infirmity, had a role in causing him to speak too soon. The flesh had taken a bow, and now he had to pay the price.

If the Lord reveals something about our future, it would be wise to hide it in our heart and wait on God to make it happen. How many times has our tongue gotten us into trouble? The enemy wants us to fail so he can shame us before God. He tried to do that with Job. The devil is a master at making a fool out of us. He is the accuser of the brethren. Even Jesus had to put Satan in his place.

> "Then saith Jesus unto him, Get thee hence, Satan: for it is written, Thou shalt worship the Lord thy God, and him only shalt thou serve." (Matt. 4:10)

The enemy's promises are all lies. We therefore need to answer, "We worship the Lord thy God, the God of Abraham, Isaac and Jacob." We must close and lock all doors the enemy might enter through, and thus destroy any sin in the camp. Do we have forbidden idols? Are we doing something that is in violation of God's laws? Is there someone we have not forgiven? Do we have continuous strife in our home? Does our heart condemn us? Are we trying to hide something from God? Do we watch sin—nature films? Have we repented of all sin and asked God for forgiveness? Have we, by faith, protected our heart by applying the Blood of the Lamb of God over the door post of our heart? Are we praying and binding the enemy from those we love?

In the book of Jonah, the mariners looked for the cause of why terrible things were happening. They took action to eliminate the problem because they feared God's judgment. Judgment sometimes falls on the just as well as the unjust, if it is not dealt with.

> "Now the word of the Lord came unto Jonah the son of Amittai, saying, Arise, go to Nineveh, that great city, and cry against it; for their wickedness is come up before me. But Jonah rose up to flee unto Tarshish from the presence of the Lord, and went down to Joppa; and he found a ship going to Tarshish: so he paid the fare thereof, and went down into it, to go with them unto Tarshish from the presence of the Lord.
>
> "But the Lord sent out a great wind into the sea, and there was a mighty tempest in the sea, so that the ship was like to be broken. Then the mariners were afraid, and cried every man unto his god, and cast forth the wares that were in the ship into the sea, to

lighten it of them. But Jonah was gone down into the sides of the ship; and he lay, and was fast asleep.

"So the shipmaster came to him, and said unto him, What meanest thou, O sleeper? arise, call upon thy God, if so be that God will think upon us, that we perish not. And they said everyone to his fellow, Come, and let us cast lots, that we may know for whose cause this evil is upon us. So they cast lots, and the lot fell upon Jonah. Then said they unto him, Tell us, we pray thee, for whose cause this evil is upon us; What is thine occupation? and whence comest thou? what is thy country? and of what people art thou?

"And he said unto them, I am an Hebrew; and I fear the Lord, the God of heaven, which hath made the sea and the dry land. Then were the men exceedingly afraid, and said unto him, Why hast thou done this? For the men knew that he fled from the presence of the Lord, because he had told them. Then said they unto him, What shall we do unto thee, that the sea may be calm unto us? for the sea wrought, and was tempestuous. And he said unto them, Take me up, and cast me forth into the sea; so shall the sea be calm unto you: for I know that for my sake this great tempest is upon you.

"Nevertheless the men rowed hard to bring it to the land; but they could not: for the sea wrought, and was tempestuous against them. Wherefore they cried

> <u>unto the Lord, and said, We beseech thee, O Lord, we beseech thee, let us not perish for this man's life, and lay not upon us innocent blood: for thou, O Lord, hast done as it pleased thee. So they took up Jonah, and cast him forth into the sea: and the sea ceased from her raging. Then the men feared the Lord exceedingly, and offered a sacrifice unto the Lord, and made vows." (Jonah 1:1-16)</u>

The devil and his messenger, the accuser of the brethren, would not stop buffeting Paul. You're not an apostle. You're a liar. You're a false witness. If you were an apostle of Jesus Christ, all the Lord's disciples would know that you are one. Rejection makes a web of faith inside the secret behind Paul's thorn in the flesh.

> <u>"Am I not an apostle? Am I not free? Have I not seen Jesus Christ our Lord? Are not ye my work in the Lord? If I be not an apostle unto others, yet doubtless I am to you: for the seal of mine apostleship are ye in the Lord." (1 Cor. 9:1-2)</u>

Paul searched his heart for truth. Why was this happening to him? He agonized over what to do. But he **was** called to be an apostle of Jesus Christ! **The call** was now pricking him towards **the call**, yet, why was he not accepted? He was now feeling condemnation for what he said to the followers of

Christ—that he was an apostle of Jesus Christ—and it could be used against him. He had no approval and no credentials from the apostles or the church to prove his calling.

There were five things working in Paul's heart that pricked the flesh:

1) **The call** of God that he was to be an apostle of Jesus Christ.
2) **The rejection** of the disciples of Christ, the church.
3) **The vow or announcement, "I am an apostle of Jesus Christ,"** that he made to the followers of Christ.
4) **Satan's messenger** buffeting him with accusations of not being an apostle now that he had been rejected.
5) **The pillars of the church**—Peter, James and John—who would be the ones to agree that he was an apostle.

The rejection brought the thorn in the flesh into focus, because he spoke too soon before he was accepted as an apostle, making him out to be a liar—but he wasn't lying, because he was an apostle by the call of God. **The call** became the major component of the thorn in the flesh pricking him toward the call. He knew that to be effective as an apostle, the other apostles would need to agree with him; but they didn't at this critical time in Jerusalem. Shaken by the rejection, the disciples' cold reception and the messenger's voice of accusations, he decided to pray for answers.

PAUL'S PRAYERS

"For this thing I besought the Lord thrice, that it might depart from me." (2 Cor. 12:8)

Now, it is very clear that **Paul did not pray against the call**; he prayed **for the call to come to fruition**. The call to be known as an apostle of Jesus Christ is what he was yearning for and waiting for the fulfillment of.

"I press toward the mark for the prize of the high calling of God in Christ Jesus." (Phil. 3:14)

If he had been accepted as an apostle of Jesus Christ by Peter, James and John, the pillars of the church, **there would have been no pricking of a thorn in the flesh.** But as he soon discovered, the only way the thorn in the flesh could not be felt was for him to crucify the flesh and walk in **the law of the Spirit of life in Christ** where there is no condemnation, showing the grace of God so that he would be accepted as an apostle. The rejection initialized the thorn. However, as time passed, **the call surpassed** rejection as the thorn.

Being rejected is devastating—it's a terrible blow. For instance, divorce is total rejection. Where once was the joy of a family and children, plans and hope—suddenly there's nothing but silence and empty space in every direction. It's like a huge vacuum has sucked out all purpose and there's no home. It's stunning. But it's awakening! "What must I do now" is the question. Jesus has the answer in the measure of the call.

The rejection got Paul's undivided attention. The only thing left to do was get down on his knees and humbly pray for God to show him what to do.

Many come to find God through rejection. God is the only hope left. Paul called out to God in prayer. By following the heart of Paul and what he was seeking, we know Paul's first prayer could have been somewhat comparable to the following:

FIRST PRAYER

"Father in heaven, I need to bring something to your attention. When I was in the Arabian Desert you gave me those mighty visions and revelations. In the visions, Lord, you showed me that I was an apostle of Jesus Christ. Lord, I'm here in Jerusalem with Peter, who I thought would be helpful in arranging to make the apostleship official. I need a letter to prove to all who would question my authority as an apostle. I need the apostles to agree to the apostleship. Dear Lord, I feel that without this letter I will in no way be considered an apostle.

"Lord I have given my testimony about my conversion to Peter, and I pray he will agree that you have called me to be an apostle of Jesus Christ. I pray that Peter, as a leader and spokesman for the apostles, works out the necessary papers and the briefing of the other apostles. Lord, may the anointing of your mighty Spirit convince all people that the announcement of this high calling is sealed and blessed by your divine authority. In Jesus' blessed name, Amen."

He observed Peter and James intently for a sign of agreement, but there was none. After a reasonable time of waiting for God's quickening power on the disciples to agree to the apostleship, but with no reply, Paul began to pray a second time, perhaps in this fashion:

SECOND PRAYER

"Father in heaven, holy is your name. I have given you my life. You gave me the vision and those revelations. **The call** is burning in my heart. Lord, I am ready to deliver the message of Jesus, of the cross and His resurrection. Lord, in my heart I know the apostleship needs to be approved soon, or I will have become a fool for speaking that day to the followers of Christ. Lord, I want you to know I am hurting—

the pain is getting stronger. Surely you have the answer on the way. Lord, thank you for making **the call** official and removing the thorn in my flesh. In Jesus' Holy name I pray, Amen."

In between the prayers, Paul waited for an answer. His heart was on the things that God had called him to do. He may have thought for a moment on the words Christ spoke to him on the Damascus road. He then decided to make one last appeal to his heavenly Father. In desperation, he may have prayed almost like this:

THIRD PRAYER

"Dear Father in heaven, I don't see any sign that I will be approved as an apostle of Jesus Christ. Lord, they know that I imprisoned and beat in every synagogue them that believed on thee. That's why I need a letter of commendation.

"I know the vision was from you and I know you cannot lie. Lord, forgive me for speaking too soon. I thought I was already an apostle when I spoke to the followers of Christ that I was an apostle—that's why I said that I was an apostle. Lord, forgive me for this error, but you did call me to be an apostle. Lord, that's what I am then! I believe you.

"Father, I pray Peter will be able to locate John. Then let John, together with Peter, persuade James to give me the letter of commendation which says, 'Paul of Tarsus, an apostle of Jesus Christ.' Father, I have prayed three times for the thorn to be removed by being accepted by Peter, James and John. Lord, in thy name I pray, Amen."

The Lord responds:

> "And he said unto me, **My grace is sufficient for thee: for my strength is made perfect in weakness.** Most gladly therefore will I rather glory in my infirmities, that the power of Christ may rest upon me. Therefore I take pleasure in infirmities, in reproaches, in necessities, in persecutions, in distresses for Christ's sake: for when I am weak, then am I strong." (2 Cor. 12:9-10)

In Galatians 1:15-18, Paul wrote of being called of God and the sequences of the Arabian Desert and Damascus; and meeting Peter and James for the first time in Jerusalem. He tried to join the disciples as an apostle and was rejected (Acts 9:26). It would be unthinkable not to go to prayer after being rejected. The urgency of fulfilling the call of God (exceeding the rejection) made it necessary to pray the three prayers.

Paul's third prayer was made from the temple in Jerusalem. We know this by knowing what his thorn was and by searching the Scriptures to find the place where the disciples rejected him (Acts 9:26). In Acts 22:17-19, we find Paul giving testimony of that day in Jerusalem. He was in the temple in a trance (ecstasy).

"And it came to pass, that, when I was come again to Jerusalem, even while I prayed in the temple, I was in a trance; And saw him saying unto me, Make haste, and get thee quickly out of Jerusalem: for they will not receive thy testimony concerning me. And I said, Lord, they know that I imprisoned and beat in every synagogue them that believed on thee:" (Acts 22:17-19)

"And he was with them coming in and going out at Jerusalem. And he spake boldly in the name of the Lord Jesus, and disputed against the Grecians: but they went about to slay him. Which when the brethren knew, they brought him down to Caesarea, and sent him forth to Tarsus." (Acts 9:28-30)

THE VOW

When Paul agreed with God to be an apostle of Jesus Christ, it became a **vow** to the Lord. When he said, "I am an apostle of Jesus Christ," that was a **vow**. It was a promise to God that he would live up to the conditions of the office. It bound him to service for life.

> "When thou shalt vow a vow unto the Lord thy God, thou shalt not slack to pay it: for the Lord thy God will surely require it of thee; and it would be sin in thee." (Deut. 23:21)

John the Baptist lost his head because Herod made an oath that he could not alter or break.

> "And he sware unto her, Whatsoever thou shalt ask of me, I will give it thee, unto the half of my kingdom. And she went forth, and said unto her mother, What

> shall I ask? And she said, The head of John the Baptist.
>
> "And she came in straightway with haste unto the king, and asked, saying, I will that thou give me by and by in a charger the head of John the Baptist. And the king was exceeding sorry; yet for his oath's sake, and for their sakes which sat with him, he would not reject her.
>
> "And immediately the king sent an executioner, and commanded his head to be brought: and he went and beheaded him in the prison, And brought his head in a charger, and gave it to the damsel: and the damsel gave it to her mother." (Mark 6:23-28)

In Bible times, a vow or promise was faithfully honored. But today, it seems there is no fear of God to keep vows or promises. The world is full of promise breakers. In the days when a man's word was highly valued, a handshake on a contract was all that was needed. The handshake sealed the agreement. It didn't require a lawyer. Where are the promise keepers?

> "For when God made promise to Abraham, because he could swear by no greater, he sware by himself, Saying, Surely blessing I will bless thee, and multiplying I will multiply thee." (Heb. 6:13-14)

Many business agreements turn sour because of broken promises. What has happened to integrity? Where does honor live? We have become a society of irresponsible people that fail to keep their word. The value of keeping a promise is immeasurable. It is a godly character.

> "The just man walketh in his integrity: his children are blessed after him." (Prov 20:7)

One of my employees opened a bank account in another state using a check made out to my company. It may have totaled $25,000 worth of Bibles. I discovered the secret account when there were just a few hundred dollars left in the account. He was fired! He was once my teacher in a Bible college class. What happened to his vow to God? It revealed his true character. He was a man without integrity.

> "Better is the poor that walketh in his integrity, than he that is perverse in his lips, and is a fool." (Prov. 19:1)

Families are falling apart everywhere because of broken vows. The marriage ceremony witnessed by family and friends was just a weak moment in their life, and so they have reconsidered. The marriage vow means nothing to them as they move on to another partner. It's called recycled relationships to whom—you guessed it—they make the same vow.

The first oath became a lie, so what happens to the next? Will not the next vow be broken likewise?

Our character is only as good as our word. Truth is: the only thing that counts in life is faith working through love. It is our testimony read by others revealing how much we are committed to God by living what the Bible teaches.

> "And Paul after this tarried there yet a good while, and then took his leave of the brethren, and sailed thence into Syria, and with him Priscilla and Aquila; having shorn his head in Cenchrea: for he had a vow." (Acts 18:18)

At another time in Jerusalem, Paul joined into a vow with four men. It was to show James, the elders and the Jews that he kept the law. Perhaps he had been too forceful in preaching salvation by grace through faith, while showing that circumcision is not the way to God.

> "Do therefore this that we say to thee: We have four men which have a vow on them; Them take, and purify thyself with them, and be at charges with them, that they may shave their heads: and all may know that those things, whereof they were informed concerning thee, are nothing; but that thou thyself also walkest orderly, and keepest the law.

"As touching the Gentiles which believe, we have written and concluded that they observe no such thing, save only that they keep themselves from things offered to idols, and from blood, and from strangled, and from fornication. Then Paul took the men, and the next day purifying himself with them entered into the temple, to signify the accomplishment of the days of purifcation, until that an offering should be offered for every one of them." (Acts 21:23-26)

PAUL'S WEAKNESS REVEALED

Human weakness is the stage for divine strength. God called Job a perfect man, yet his weakness was a lack of the knowledge of God. Paul's weakness was a lack of the **foreknowledge of** God. If Paul had had foreknowledge of God, he would have known the disciples would reject him. He knew God called him as an apostle, but he didn't know the day of its recognition. He believed it, but God had a special way of working it out for His glory. Thus, he had to hang on to the call!

When Paul was in Jerusalem at that time, he only saw Peter and James. He really wanted to be recognized as an apostle as soon as possible. Yet, they certainly weren't going to do something without John's approval, and he didn't see John on this trip. But how else could he preach the Gospel effectively without some type of credentials from the church?

When he was persecuting the Christians, he had letters from the High Priest as proof of his authority.

> "And Saul, yet breathing out threatenings and slaughter against the disciples of the Lord, went unto the high priest, And **desired of him letters** to Damascus to the synagogues, that if he found any of this way, whether they were men or women, he might bring them bound unto Jerusalem." (Acts 9:1-2)

Paul began to sort out **the call** in his mind, heart and soul. He sought the Lord all the more. He began to distance himself from the flesh. He wanted to please the Lord; **the call** was always on his mind.

The Lord seems to always send a friend to give support in the time of trouble. In Paul's case, it was Barnabas; and so Barnabas emerges as one trying to convince the apostles of Paul's calling.

> "But Barnabas took him, and brought him to the apostles, and declared unto them how he had seen the Lord in the way, and that he had spoken to him, and how he had preached boldly at Damascus in the name of Jesus." (Acts 9:27)

Barnabas believed in Paul with conviction. However, it was very little consolation to the stunning rejection of the disciples. Soon Paul had to leave Jerusalem and perhaps went to Tarsus discouraged, because the Grecians were a threatening force that was about to kill him.

In the Book of Titus, Paul condemns the Grecians over their abominable character.

> "For there are many unruly and vain talkers and deceivers, specially they of the circumcision: Whose mouths must be stopped, who subvert whole houses, teaching things which they ought not, for filthy lucre's sake.
>
> "One of themselves, even a prophet of their own, said, The Cretians are alway liars, evil beasts, slow bellies. This witness is true. Wherefore rebuke them sharply, that they may be sound in the faith; Not giving heed to Jewish fables, and commandments of men, that turn from the truth.
>
> "Unto the pure all things are pure: but unto them that are defiled and unbelieving is nothing pure; but even their mind and conscience is defiled. They profess that they know God; but in works they deny him, being abominable, and disobedient, and unto every good work reprobate." (Titus 1:10-16)

The Lord provides ample time and warning for the sinner to repent. How would we get saved without time and grace from the Lord? He takes our weakness, our ego and our limitations, and shows us what we need to be by the light of His Holy Word.

Grace is not getting what we deserve, so that divine assistance can shape and mold us in God's time by regeneration and sanctification.

> "He hath not dealt with us after our sins; nor rewarded us according to our iniquities." (Ps 103:10)

Sanctification works like a **flesh-light** to reveal the sin nature that's in us—those things that are not pleasing to God. It urges us to repent and forsake sinful living and to get more acquainted with spiritual living.

> "That ye put off concerning the former conversation the old man, which is corrupt according to the deceitful lusts; And be renewed in the spirit of your mind; And that ye put on the new man, which after God is created in righteousness and true holiness." (Eph. 4:22-24)
>
> "Put on the whole armour of God, that ye may be able to stand against the wiles of the devil. For we wrestle not against flesh and blood, but against principalities, against powers, against the rulers of the darkness of this world, against spiritual wickedness in high places." (Eph. 6:11-12)

EGOTISM

Egotism is one of the conditions that comes from infirmity, and since they're linked, we'll give Merriam-Webster's 11th Collegiate Dictionary's meaning of them together:

Infirmity:

1. The quality or state of being infirm. The condition of being feeble; frailty; disease; malady; a personal failing: foible; one of the besetting infirmities of living creatures is egotism—A. J. Toynbee.

Egotism:

1 a: excessive use of the first person singular personal pronoun.
  b: the practice of talking about oneself too much.
2. an exaggerated sense of self-importance.

No one is exempt from a **personal failing** or weakness—egotism. We have seen this displayed in the media, in the world and in the church.

What pastor is not motivated greatly by the call to preach the Word? It's exciting when you're called to represent the Lord in some capacity in ministry: as a pastor, teacher, missionary, etc. At what level, on a scale of 1 to 100, was the motivation factor for Paul when God called him to be an apostle of Jesus Christ? It went off the chart! He was ready to search for the lost sheep the day he was called to be an apostle, for it is the highest calling of God to lead people to Christ.

Most beloved pastors and teachers start out in the ministry with some degree of **ego**. It's almost natural to talk about what God has revealed that He is going to do in your ministry.

In the beginning of Paul's ministry, he also could have spent unnecessary time thinking about himself. This would be an infirmity—a weakness and trial in the flesh. He wanted to prove himself to the disciples, too. Moreover, knowing that God had given him the task to write the Word was the most motivated moment of his life. It was something he could not lay aside for another day. Yet, the Word came while following the dictates of the Holy Spirit as he lived in the measure of the call.

When the disciples walked with Jesus on earth, some of their comments were self-serving. They didn't have a book titled, How to Speak Without an Excelling Ego; or a book teaching, Ten Ways on How to Stay Humble.

This is a weakness many of us have from time to time. We want to feel important to those around us. So, at times, our conversations are just a little too much about "me." I want to hear about me. Don't you see me? I want to be me. It takes a lot of practice for me to put down me. The flesh is a person and alive; sometimes as physical, carnal or just plain natural—flesh. The problem is me-consciousness.

> "For I say, through the grace given unto me, to every man that is among you, not to think of himself more highly than he ought to think; but to think soberly, according as God hath dealt to every man the measure of faith." (Rom. 12:3)

Willis Hamm, a good friend of mine, mentioned that sometimes while performing, he has gotten caught up in the moment of thinking how good it is; and soon after—a word or a line in the song is forgotten.

In a repentant way, he said he thinks one cause is ego. I agreed—it's happened to me, too. Ego is stealthy; it's a silent setback. It's the cause of memory loss or some other weakness of the flesh. It will cause attention deficit disorder. No matter how much we try, no one can be perfect in the flesh. The perfection zone is at the cross and the law of the Spirit of life in Christ. Oh, but the flesh is just waiting to act. It cries out for recognition. All people live with it, the infirmity of the flesh. It's a weakness.

Sometimes a line is forgotten because of distraction—self-consciousness and me-consciousness instead of Christ-consciousness. It's not being focused in Christ, or it could be just not being prepared. It is like a water line—the weakest spot in the line is where it will spring a leak or break under high pressure. This teaches us we must work more on the weak areas of our life, making our character stronger and living the Word. We always feel we could have done better. That's infirmity of the flesh!

If we get caught up into thinking how good or perfect we sound, in a flash we may not remember the next line. It's something that comes against the knowledge of God. That's ego!

> "For though we walk in the flesh, we do not war after the flesh: (For the weapons of our warfare are not carnal, but mighty through God to the pulling down of strong holds;) Casting down imaginations, and every high thing that exalteth itself against the knowledge of God, and bringing into captivity every thought to the obedience of Christ;" (2 Cor. 10:3-5)

All thoughts and imaginations that come to our mind that lift up self in any manner must be cast down immediately. It's the old sin nature that tempts us to glorify self. We must be cross-conscious, Christ-conscious and to God be the glory-conscious.

> "Thou wast perfect in thy ways from the day that thou wast created, till iniquity was found in thee. By the multitude of thy merchandise they have filled the midst of thee with violence, and thou hast sinned: therefore I will cast thee as profane out of the mountain of God: and I will destroy thee, O covering cherub, from the midst of the stones of fire." (Ezek. 28:15-16)

It was pride through the merchandise that brought down Satan. God gives us the ability to write beautiful Gospel songs that have a powerful effect on others; but they must be channeled back to God to give Him the glory. We are tempted to think that it is by something we did. The very thought that we did it will bring about our fall, so we must ask the Lord to shield us from ego and pride. To keep the anointing in ministry, it is required that Jesus be Lord.

> "Wherefore let him that thinketh he standeth take heed lest he fall." (1 Cor. 10:12)

In the house of God, the Lord will not bless or honor ego or pride. The very thought of your personal impact made by the greatness of your song, voice or spoken word will cause a crash and burn. The Lord will humble you! So we must rely on the grace of God. His grace is sufficient. The call to live in Christ is made real here.

It is a <u>temptation</u> to abide in the flesh and meditate on self. It is self-consciousness instead of Christ-consciousness. Was Paul thinking back to the days he first started preaching, and now he has matured in the Word in a deeper way? His ego may have showed <u>the trial of the flesh</u>; but time and grace, working with the knowledge of God's Holy Word, brought wisdom and humility. Hence, we will have fewer errors caused by ego if we keep our focus on lifting up Jesus while putting down self. The safety zone is in the law of the Spirit of life in Christ and Jesus being glorified.

> <u>"But God forbid that I should glory, save in the cross of our Lord Jesus Christ, by whom the world is crucified unto me, and I unto the world." (Gal 6:14)</u>

Ego could have been expressed by Paul at the beginning of his ministry because it would naturally show up after some of God's mighty miracles. People understandably bring it about with glowing compliments. But all glory and praise must be channeled to the Lord.

> <u>"But I will come to you shortly, if the Lord will, and will know, not the speech of them which are puffed</u>

up, but the power. For the kingdom of God is not in word, but in power." (1 Cor. 4:19-20)

When the rejection happened, that was the beginning of the messenger of Satan making buffeting accusations against Paul of not being an apostle. One of the buffeting remarks from Satan could have been ego. It is the kind of personality that Satan is a master of. But the call blocked the buffeting words that did not measure up to the character of the Word. Oh, yes, and thank the Lord, the thorn in the flesh, **the call**, circumcised Paul's heart. It sensitized his lips to wait upon the Holy Spirit before speaking, and to pray without ceasing.

"Though I might also have confidence in the flesh. If any other man thinketh that he hath whereof he might trust in the flesh, I more: Circumcised the eighth day, of the stock of Israel, of the tribe of Benjamin, an Hebrew of the Hebrews; as touching the law, a Pharisee; Concerning zeal, persecuting the church; touching the righteousness which is in the law, blameless.

"But what things were gain to me, those I counted loss for Christ. Yea doubtless, and I count all things but loss for the excellency of the knowledge of Christ Jesus my Lord: for whom I have suffered the loss of all things, and do count them but dung, that I may win Christ, And be found in him, not having mine own righteousness, which is of the law, but that which is through the faith of Christ, the righteousness which is of God by faith:

"That I may know him, and the power of his resurrection, and the fellowship of his sufferings, being made conformable unto his death; If by any means I might attain unto the resurrection of the dead.

"Not as though I had already attained, either were already perfect: but I follow after, if that I may apprehend that for which also I am apprehended of Christ Jesus. Brethren, I count not myself to have apprehended: but this one thing I do, forgetting those things which are behind, and reaching forth unto those things which are before, I press toward the mark for the prize of the high calling of God in Christ Jesus.

"Let us therefore, as many as be perfect, be thus minded: and if in anything ye be otherwise minded, God shall reveal even this unto you. Nevertheless, whereto we have already attained, let us walk by the same rule, let us mind the same thing. Brethren, be followers together of me, and mark them which walk so as ye have us for an ensample." (Phil. 3:4-17)

With the urgency to be recognized as an apostle soon, Paul learned to live faultless in character and mirrored the Word he represented. How was he going to be accepted by the church if he didn't show he was blameless, being in the divine character of Jesus Christ? He had to live where there is no condemnation. How could he write the Holy Word of God and not be transformed and changed into the image of Jesus Christ?

This would take fasting, special prayer and godly planning. He would need to seek the Holy Spirit intimately for what to say and how to present himself as an author of God's Holy Word.

It was then that his words flowed out to all, being sanctified by prayer and anointed by the Lordship of Jesus Christ. He had to have spiritual depth in God and insight to be Holy and perfect. He had spiritual knowledge inspired by God. He lived hidden in the cross of Christ. He knew the complete scope of its importance. He worked to exalt Christ while living in humility.

The call kept pricking him to live in the character and measure of the Word. He knew he had to do whatever it took to be accepted and recognized as an apostle of Jesus Christ. So that nothing would hinder the recognition, Paul trusted God to remove any character flaw the Holy Spirit revealed or convicted him of.

> "If a man therefore purge himself from these, he shall be a vessel unto honour, sanctified, and meet for the master's use, and prepared unto every good work." (2 Tim. 2:21)

The question might be asked, "What's on your mind?"

Mike Payne and Ronnie Hinson wrote a beautiful song, When He Was on the Cross I Was on His Mind, and what's interesting is how the song begins: "I'm not on an **ego trip**; I'm nothing on my own. I make mistakes, and often slip just common flesh and bones. But I'll prove someday just what I say—I'm of a special kind—when he was on the cross, I was on His mind."

So it was with Paul—he knew he was not on an ego trip. He was called to be an apostle of Jesus Christ. He now realized the weakness of the flesh of speaking too soon. He also knew that God was omniscient and foreknew what would happen in Jerusalem. He had to press on in the call. Yet, Paul had to wait for God's appointed time, knowing the grace of God would eventually work out the apostleship.

Who can master **ego** or tame the tongue? When our name is mentioned, it is not normal to bow our head and pray that **ego** will not be seen in me.

> "Even so the tongue is a little member, and boasteth great things. Behold, how great a matter a little fire kindleth!
>
> "And the tongue is a fire, a world of iniquity: so is the tongue among our members, that it defileth the whole body, and setteth on fire the course of nature; and it is set on fire of hell.

"For every kind of beasts, and of birds, and of serpents, and of things in the sea, is tamed, and hath been tamed of mankind: But the tongue can no man tame; it is an unruly evil, full of deadly poison.

"Therewith bless we God, even the Father; and therewith curse we men, which are made after the similitude of God." (James 3:5-9)

The cool carnal lip thing has invaded many of our youth today; the Bible calls them "a froward person". It means habitually disposed to disobedience and opposition. It is what the Bible predicted would come in the last days.

It is easily concluded that the flesh is characterized by feebleness, weakness, disease and egotism. However, the believer, walking in the Word and yielding to the dictates of the Holy Spirit, has everything needed to keep ego from ruining the testimony of Christ in him.

Super Bowl XLI was won by the Indianapolis Colts who were coached by Tony Dungy. He did the unusual—he gave the glory to God! His is one of the most amazing testimonies I have ever witnessed. The sports announcers say that Dungy is calm and seemingly unflappable. His players say he never yells or tries to intimidate. He never uses profanity and has no apparent ego.

This is a rarity in sports. It is obvious that Dungy has a deep personal relationship with Jesus Christ from the words he speaks and the testimonies of those around him. He has undoubtedly found that ego can be controlled, eliminated, shut out, dismissed, ejected and evicted, by being reminded of the call of God to live in the character of Christ, in measure and in the Word.

> "Let another man praise thee, and not thine own mouth; a stranger, and not thine own lips." (Prov. 27:2)

Tony Dungy stands out as the kind of role-model our young men and women need. His character shows that he has a deep respect for, and a godly fear of the Lord.

> "The fear of the LORD is to hate evil: pride, and arrogancy, and the evil way, and the froward mouth, do I hate." (Prov. 8:13)

Godly fear causes us to live retrospectively in honor to the author of our faith. We gain a wealth of inspirational strength as we meditate on our bed at night—on our wrongs and how to make more things right.

> There's a song that I have sung many times at nursing homes, Did I Make a Difference. It has a great line, "What hurts did I heal? What wrongs did I right? Did I raise my voice in defense of the truth? Did I lend my hand to the destitute?"

Many times I have witnessed the joy of agreement from the faces of the frail and lonely. The Gospel in a song does make a difference. Too many times we raise our voice in irritation or anger. When we do—it is not to advance the truth. It puts us in the Hall of Shame. On this I must reflect. Lord, "forgive me."

Oh, if we could grasp the truth—in Christ, we find awakening solutions: we can be a problem solver or a problem maker. We can make a difference. Then irritations can be resolved and the world's problems will be one less.

Something else I have learned from walking in the Word: someone's lofty compliment cannot be repeated by the recipient. It is not humble to tell another, your wife, husband, children, grandchildren or a close friend, the good things others have said about you. It is like receiving cash from highly valuable assets we no longer own. We gave our self rights to Jesus Christ at the cross and so all compliments go to Him.

It is like the seat marked VIP; you should never sit there because it is RESERVED for **EGO.**

"But when thou doest alms, let not thy left hand know what thy right hand doeth:" (Matt. 6:3)

Lest any man think of me above that which he sees me to be or hears of me, keeps ringing true. The self-sacrificing response is: point the compliment to Jesus and humbly honor and glorify His Name. We cannot accept an iota of credit, but need to quickly point to Jesus Christ as the only one deserving the honor. When personal honors are deposited to our credit account, we must make immediate transfers to His account.

It takes daily practice of denying self, while giving the glory and praise to God, so we don't get caught up on Ego Mountain. It is a very slippery, rocky place, anyhow. Remember that the dead in Christ show no signs of ego.

In the ministry of God's Word, the blessings flow out by the power of the Word. The Word encourages us to boldly live in truth and speak to the mountains of life. When we live the Gospel, we are seen as an image of Christ. We are ambassadors of the holiness of God. When we minister the Word, it demonstrates itself through power. The power of the Word in a believing heart reaches out to the needs of others by doing the works of God. It's His power that is at work—it's the Word.

> "And there sat a certain man at Lystra, impotent in his feet, being a cripple from his mother's womb, who never had walked: The same heard Paul speak: who stedfastly beholding him, and **perceiving that he had faith to be healed**, Said with a loud voice, Stand upright on thy feet. And he leaped and walked.
>
> "And when the people saw what Paul had done, they lifted up their voices, saying in the speech of Lycaonia, The gods are come down to us in the like-

ness of men. And they called Barnabas, Jupiter; and Paul, Mercurius, because he was the chief speaker. Then the priest of Jupiter, which was before their city, brought oxen and garlands unto the gates, and would have done sacrifice with the people.

"Which when the apostles, Barnabas and Paul, heard of, they rent their clothes, and ran in among the people, crying out, And saying, Sirs, why do ye these things? We also are men of like passions with you, and preach unto you that ye should turn from these vanities unto the living God, which made heaven, and earth, and the sea, and all things that are therein:" (Acts 14:8-15)

The priest started preparing a sacrifice and worship service to honor and worship Paul and Barnabas because of the miracle that happened when Paul said to the cripple, "stand upright on thy feet." It got the priest excited, thinking he was visited by gods. He didn't know these were ordinary men that God worked the miracle through.

It was the signs and wonders that follow the Word, but they gave Paul and Barnabas all the glory and credit for it. Paul and Barnabas would have none of it. They were wrought with anguish and responded immediately with humility to put down the flesh, ego and pride, giving the glory to God.

I was singing a song, "The Old Man Is Dead" in a large church of perhaps two thousand people in Tennessee several years ago, and right in the middle of the song, a woman screamed out real loud. A year later I was told what happened. She had smoked cigarettes for over twenty years and the Lord set her free from that filthy weed through that song. It was the anointing of the Word in the song that set her free. I was just the vessel the Lord used. All the glory belongs to God alone.

Why don't more people claim the promises of God for victory over temptation?

> "There hath no temptation taken you but such as is common to man: but God is faithful, who will not suffer you to be tempted above that ye are able; but will with the temptation also make a way to escape, that ye may be able to bear it." (1 Cor 10:13)

For ministries to be in proper character, the vessel God uses must not be ostentatious, pretentious, showy, vain, arrogant or proud.

Paul must have proposed for himself to practice daily on being simple, unostentatious, unpretentious, compliant, resigned, quiet, subdued and submissive to the character of Christ in order to achieve his goal of being accepted as an apostle of Jesus Christ. In a respectful fear of God, he meditated on the things of God.

> "Meditate upon these things; give thyself wholly to them; that thy profiting may appear to all. Take heed unto thyself, and unto the doctrine; continue in them: for in doing this thou shalt both save thyself, and them that hear thee." (1 Tim. 4:15)

By meditating on the Word of God day and night, we will keep making corrections and adjustments in our lives. The Word causes us to reflect on its anointing power and the changes in life we have been brought through.

Paul lived and breathed the Gospel. Paul was held in the highest esteem by the Galatians early in his ministry. They highly honored him. Their love and dedication blessed his life. But suddenly their loyalty to the Gospel (the cross) and to him turned to weakness, worthlessness and, ultimately, bondage.

> "But now, after that ye have known God, or rather are known of God, how turn ye again to the weak and beggarly elements, whereunto ye desire again to be in bondage?" (Gal. 4:9)
>
> "Where is then the blessedness ye spake of? for I bear you record, that, if it had been possible, **ye would have plucked out your own eyes**, and have given them to me." (Gal. 4:15)

We often hear, "I'd give my right arm for that." It was possibly the same figure of speech that was used to show how dedicated they once were to Jesus Christ and the cross, but now have turned back to beggarly elements (this refers to believers turning their back on the cross and being in bondage that comes from serving the law of sin and death).

They once had such great devotion to the Gospel (the cross) and loyalty to him, a loyalty so attached to him that they would have done anything for his personal welfare. To fully describe their zeal for the Gospel (the cross) and loyalty to him, he said they would have even given him their eyes. It is an idiom. Their compliments could have made his ego soar. It was not about Paul having **poor eyesight!** It was showing a clear picture of how easy it is to fall back into following the law. The Judaizers were making the law of circumcision the way of salvation and not the cross alone. It meant bondage.

GOD WARNS THOSE WHO TURN BACK FROM THE CROSS

"It is a fearful thing to fall into the hands of the living God. But call to remembrance the former days, in which, after ye were illuminated, ye endured a great fight of afflictions; Partly, whilst ye were made a gazingstock both by reproaches and afflictions; and partly, whilst ye became companions of them that were so used.

"For ye had compassion of me in my bonds, and took joyfully the spoiling of your goods, knowing in yourselves that ye have in heaven a better and an enduring substance. Cast not away therefore your confidence, which hath great recompence of reward. For ye have need of patience, that, after ye have done the will of God, ye might receive the promise.

"For yet a little while, and he that shall come will come, and will not tarry. **Now the just shall live by faith**: but if any man draw back, my soul shall have no pleasure in him." (Heb. 10:31-38)

The Galatians were like so many today that fail to live by the law of the Spirit of life in Christ Jesus. Our justification is having faith in the finished work of Christ on the cross.

"And another also said, Lord, I will follow thee; but let me first go bid them farewell, which are at home at my house. And Jesus said unto him, No man, having put his hand to the plough, and looking back, is fit for the kingdom of God." (Luke 9:61-62)

"That which is gone out of thy lips thou shalt keep and perform; even a freewill offering, according as thou hast vowed unto the Lord thy God, which thou hast promised with thy mouth." (Deut. 23:23)

INFIRMITY AND THE TRIAL

Jesus did not say His strength is made perfect because of **people, poor eyesight, Satan's messenger, personal failures, the unknown, infirmities or physical limitations**. He said in weakness!

Webster says **Infirmity** is: 1) feeble. 2) A weakness. 3) A disease. 4) A personal failing—egotism: one of the besetting infirmities of living creatures is egotism.

> "Ye know how through **infirmity** of the flesh I preached the gospel unto you at the first. And my **temptation** which was in my flesh ye despised not, nor rejected; but received me as an **angel of God**, even as Christ Jesus." (Gal. 4:13-14)

By studying all meanings of "infirmity," we also find that egotism, conceit and troublesome things relate to the weakness of the flesh. Disappointment, the unknown and uncertainty are also linked to **infirmity**. All weaknesses come from the flesh—not the spirit.

It appears that infirmity was a common word in Bible times to show human nature and weaknesses of the natural man. You can have good health, perfect teeth, perfect feet, see and count a million stars in heaven and still have an infirmity, such as the unknown, disappointment or uncertainty. Hello flesh! Hello weakness!

The word **temptation** in this passage means **trial.** When Paul first preached the message of the cross to the Galatians, he was going through a trial of rejection of his apostleship by the disciples. However, he was extremely encouraged during this tough time because the Galatians treated him as an angel of God. **They** recognized his anointing.

We know that Paul had to be disappointed by the rejection of the disciples; so let us examine the area of his life concerning the **unknown** of the apostleship. The truth is—Paul did not come to Jerusalem to join the disciples with the foreknowledge of God. If he had the **foreknowledge** of God (that he would be rejected), he would not have gone there. He would have stayed home. He would have been like Peter and gone fishing! He would have not told anyone he was an apostle of Jesus Christ.

"And when Saul was come to Jerusalem, he assayed to join himself to the disciples: but they were all afraid of him, and believed not that he was a disciple." (Acts 9:26)

Webster says **Assayed** means: 1) Try, attempt. 2) To analyze (as an ore). 3) To judge the worth of. 4) Estimate.

It is very clear he tried to join them, but they were all afraid of him and **didn't believe he was a disciple of Christ**. Their fears brushed him off. They wouldn't look him in the eye. The enemy, the accuser of the brethren, may have suggested it was a trick to put them in prison. He was unknown as an apostle at that time.

The unknown was all around Paul. The Gospel Paul wrote wasn't handed to him from God by UPS in a 7 lb. box. It came by inspiration of the Holy Ghost as he walked in union with God. Paul wrote about living by faith as the Holy Spirit led him. Some of it came while in a jail cell, like the Book of Philemon. His life was filled of the unknown, and uncertainty.

His vision, while in paradise, most likely showed that he was going to be the author of the Gospel. But the message of the cross, the Word, came by the inspiration of the Holy Ghost and by a faith walk with God. It came moment by moment, as the Holy Ghost sent him on missionary journeys and into a remarkable prison ministry.

It takes time to comprehend the deep knowledge of the Word. God develops our character as we live the Gospel (the cross). Paul was not supernatural, but the Word was. Only

God is all-knowing: therefore, Paul had to go through times of the unknown.

We know that Paul's letters of the Bible were not written in a single day. It took **years** for the complete work of his epistles to be written.

The disciples may have rejected Paul, but the Holy Ghost did not! The Holy Ghost came into a church service in Antioch and made church history.

> "As they ministered to the Lord, and fasted, the Holy Ghost said, Separate me Barnabas and Saul (Paul) for the work whereunto I have called them. And when they had fasted and prayed, and laid their hands on them, they sent them away. So they, being sent forth by the Holy Ghost, departed unto Seleucia; and from thence they sailed to Cyprus." (Acts 13:2-4)

Jesus' followers first became known as Christians in Antioch. Also, the first missionaries, Paul and Barnabas, were sent out from Antioch to Seleucia and Cyprus by the Holy Ghost. The Holy Ghost was Paul's commander-in-chief. He quickly learned what the kingdom of God is all about.

> "For the kingdom of God is not meat and drink; but righteousness, and peace, and joy in the Holy Ghost." (Rom. 14:17)

There are many amazing demonstrations of Paul's faith and relationship with his commander-in-chief, the Holy Ghost. One that bears notice is recorded in the Book of Acts.

> "And it came to pass, that, while Apollos was at Corinth, Paul having passed through the upper coasts came to Ephesus: and finding certain disciples, He said unto them, **Have ye received the Holy Ghost since ye believed?** And they said unto him, We have not so much as heard whether there be any HolyGhost.
>
> "And he said unto them, Unto what then were ye baptized? And they said, Unto John's baptism. Then said Paul, John verily baptized with the baptism of repentance, saying unto the people, that they should believe on him which should come after him, that is, on Christ Jesus.
>
> "When they heard this, they were baptized in the name of the Lord Jesus. And when Paul had laid his hands upon them, the Holy Ghost came on them; and they spake with tongues, and prophesied." (Acts 19:1-6)

Why did Paul ask these **believers,** "Have you received the Holy Ghost since you believed?" Without doubt, the Gospel message he was hearing from them was incomplete, for they only knew of John's baptism unto repentance. They had not experienced what John foretold about Christ—that He would send the Holy Ghost.

> "I indeed baptize you with water unto repentance: but he that cometh after me is mightier than I, whose shoes I am not worthy to bear: he shall baptize you with the Holy Ghost, and with fire:" (Matt. 3:11)

Paul introduced the Holy Ghost to certain disciples who were uninformed. The unknown was made known. The sin nature (Romans chapter seven) cannot be controlled without the anointing of the Holy Ghost (Romans 8:1-2). Were they uneducated in the **law of the Spirit of life in Christ?**

The Gospel light switch that opens our hearts and minds to the Word of God is the Holy Ghost. He is the key that unlocks the truth. He is the spiritual agent that imparts spiritual knowledge and wisdom from God.

> "But the wisdom that is from above is first pure, then peaceable, gentle, and easy to be intreated, full of mercy and good fruits, without partiality, and without hypocrisy." (James 3:17)

If the switch is turned off, there is no spiritual light in the soul. There is no power connected to the camera of life. It is out of focus, fastened to a tripod that has only two legs. It falls often and never gets a clear picture of God's Holy Word or His perfect will. The Holy Ghost is the Lord's administrative agent. He inhabits the praises of His people.

GOD'S GPS

Paul's missionary journeys began at Seleucia. From there he sailed to Cyprus. Jesus gave His disciples instructions for their journeys, so Paul's journey would be no different.

> "And commanded them that they should take nothing for their journey, save a staff only; no scrip, no bread, no money in their purse:" (Mark 6:8)

The reason not to take scrip, bread or money was faith. God would be their source. Therefore, it is by faith that Paul stepped into the unknown. Faith is the key word in Paul's life. The following unlocks the secrets of the infirmity of the flesh:

When Paul wrote in Galatians, how through infirmity of the flesh I preached the Gospel unto you at the first, he was writing about his GPS position in the faith seventeen years earlier. We clearly see there is a big difference between now and back then. Don't we wish we knew back then what we know now? Paul is identifying with **his position** "back then" as being in pursuit of being accepted as an apostle of Jesus Christ by the disciples. How long would it take for them to receive him? He didn't know the day or how God would make it known. All of these questions belong to the family of infirmity: **the unknown,** disappointment and uncertainty.

But when he wrote the Book of Galatians, his position in the faith was **known**. His ministry had gone on for about seventeen years, and now He was known as an apostle of Jesus Christ. He had his diploma. He had the signs and wonders. He had the position of an apostle and was recognized by the Church. Do you see it? Do you see the trail and infirmity of the flesh, back when he didn't have the position? He was in the unknown, in weakness of the flesh, when he was saying how "through infirmity of the flesh, I preached the Gospel unto you **at the first**." He wrote the Book of Galatians after he was accepted. He was looking back and writing about what he was back then.

At the first, Paul was pointing back to when he was preaching in the unknown, in disappointment and uncertain of whether he would be accepted as an apostle of Jesus Christ or had run the race in vain.

> "Then fourteen years after I went up again to Jerusalem with Barnabas, and took Titus with me also. And I went up by revelation, and communicated

> unto them that gospel which I preach among the Gentiles, but privately to them which were of reputation, **lest by any means I should run, or had run, in vain**." (Gal. 2:1-2)

This is where, how through infirmity of the flesh I preached the gospel unto you **at the first**, is fully understood. It was the unknown—it was the uncertain back then—but not now! The substance of things hoped for had come to fruition. It was in his right hand. He had his graduation diploma to prove his apostleship. We will see later in this book that he was approved! He was commemorated. The announcement became global. He became known not as Saul, the persecutor of the church, but Paul, an apostle of Jesus Christ.

Therefore, we have **faith** as the new order to follow:

> "But without faith it is impossible to please him: for he that cometh to God must believe that he is, and that he is a rewarder of them that diligently seek him." (Heb. 11:6)

To please God we must believe in Jesus Christ and walk by faith.

Living by faith causes us to be willing to yield to the Spirit over and over until it becomes second nature. We eventually learn the value of not objecting to change so we don't have to feel pain and suffer hurt before we change.

It is learning to listen for the soft voice of Holy Spirit and doing what is asked of us. The more we submit, the more we become supple. When God sees our willingness to serve humbly, the closer we become in union with the Holy Spirit, and the more the unknown is fully known. Thus, we walk in the light: in abundance, in truth and in knowledge.

If someone is living in rebellion to God's Word, truth and knowledge are hidden from them, and sometimes from their children as well. They go about life ignorant, stumbling, groping in darkness and falling into pits. Their pockets have holes and their finances sift like the sand of the sea through their fingers. They are in one relationship after another, blaming others for their failures. It is all because of unbelief of the Word that they walk through life hurt, discouraged and sad. Their lives are robbed day after day. They never enjoy the wealth and peace of God.

These kinds of people are never able to discern solutions to their problems. They try to buy the answers through secular counselors. But it just brings more deception that builds higher walls around them to keep them in prison longer. They are robbed of happiness and the abundant life. Satan's cunning plan for them must be broken by complete surrender to Christ by way of the cross.

The simple way of turning it all around in Christ is to invite the Holy Spirit to guide you in truth. When we are in obedience to the truth of God's Word, the truth turns on a light and darkness disappears. God's Word reveals the way to true happiness and joy. Make yourself available for God to show you His will for your life.

> "And I, brethren, when I came to you, came not with excellency of speech or of wisdom, declaring unto you the testimony of God. For I determined not to know anything among you, save Jesus Christ, and him crucified. And I was with you in weakness, and in fear, and in much trembling. And my speech and my preaching was not with enticing words of man's wisdom, but in demonstration of the Spirit and of power: That your faith should not stand in the wisdom of men, but in the power of God." (1 Cor. 2:1-5)

I have heard of pastors being in the pulpit for many years and then realizing that they were never called of God. It was just something that they thought they might like to do. This would be a solid case for the preaching of the Gospel through the wisdom of men. They are not called of God, and there is no anointing or connection with the cross and the Holy Spirit in their message. The wisdom of men is missing God's anointing and demonstration of the power of the Holy Spirit.

> "For Christ sent me not to baptize, but to preach the gospel: not with wisdom of words, lest the cross of Christ should be made of none effect." (1 Cor 1:17)

Many seek out this kind of powerless church so their sin can remain dormant and hidden while having a seared conscious. They don't want to be bothered by the soul-cleansing message of the cross, God's Word in power and demonstration. They want to be comfortable living in sin nature and never moving closer to a Holy God. One thing is for sure—the Holy Spirit is not welcomed there.

I am sure Paul renewed his faith over and over by the promises of God, and the call of God continually renewed his position in the faith. Without a doubt, he could not forget that glorious meeting in the church at Antioch and what the Holy Ghost said: Separate me Barnabas and Saul (Paul) for the work whereunto I have called them.

A good analogy of what the Holy Ghost is to a faithful servant of God, following the purpose and will of God, is the **GPS** systems in our cars of today. A computer screen on the dash of the car displays a map of our current position (faith).

Before we begin the journey, we enter the address of our destination (heaven) and a voice comes over the car audio speakers and tells us what street or highway to take. If we make a wrong turn along the route, it redirects us to the nearest street that leads us back to the (straight and narrow) way of our destination.

Recently, my wife and I were taking Shawn, our grandson, on a trip into the mountains. After an hour of driving on a up and down highway, the voice on the GPS system instructed us to turn left at the next light in about ½ mile. It is amazing that a satellite in the sky is used to accurately pinpoint our current location, no matter where we are. It is a wonderful example of our all-knowing and all-seeing God.

THE WORD OF WISDOM – THE WORD OF KNOWLEDGE

In Antioch, when the Holy Ghost spoke to the believers, He spoke through an office (GPS) of the church. A prophet gave a word of wisdom (information—something to know and do) and a word of knowledge (information—something to know that is past tense) to the believers who were there. Here are the **prophets** and **teachers** who were on the scene:

> "Now there were in the church that was at Antioch certain prophets and teachers; as Barnabas, and Simeon that was called Niger, and Lucius of Cyrene, and Manaen, which had been brought up with Herod the tetrarch, and Saul." (Acts 13:1)
>
> "Surely the Lord God will do nothing, but he revealeth his secret unto his servants the prophets." (Amos 3:7)

The following is a word of wisdom (information—something to do) that the Holy Ghost gave Agabus, a prophet, to tell Paul what was going to happen to him in Jerusalem. It was to prepare him for what was coming, and it came to pass just as the prophet said it would.

> "And as we tarried there many days, there came down from Judaea a certain prophet, named Agabus. And when he was come unto us, he took Paul's girdle, and bound his own hands and feet, and said, Thus saith the Holy Ghost, So shall the Jews at Jerusalem bind the man that owneth this girdle, and shall deliver him into the hands of the Gentiles." (Acts 21:10-11)

The Holy Spirit gave Philip a word of wisdom (something to know and do), for He sent him into Gaza to help an Ethiopian be saved and baptized with water.

> "Then the Spirit said unto Philip, Go near, and join thyself to this chariot." (Acts 8:29)
>
> "And Philip said, If thou believest with all thine heart, thou mayest. And he answered and said, I believe that Jesus Christ is the Son of God. And he commanded the chariot to stand still: and they went down both into the water, both Philip and the eunuch; and he baptized him." (Acts 8:37-38)

"And he said, Hear now my words: If there be a prophet among you, I the Lord will make myself known unto him in a vision, and will speak unto him in a dream. My servant Moses is not so, who is faithful in all mine house. With him will I speak mouth to mouth, even apparently, and not in dark speeches; and the similitude of the Lord shall he behold: wherefore then were ye not afraid to speak against my servant Moses?" (Num. 12:6-8)

PAUL TELLS HOW THE WORD CAME TO HIM

"All Scripture is given by inspiration of God, and is profitable for doctrine, for reproof, for correction, for instruction in righteousness: That the man of God may be perfect, throughly furnished unto all good works." (2 Tim. 3:16-17)

Thus, in the beginning of Paul's ministry, the unknowns were made known to him by inspiration of the Holy Spirit. Paul, in turn, used the gifts of the Spirit to minister to others by the testimony of his life in Christ, by a word of wisdom (something to know and do) or a word of knowledge (something to know), as the Holy Spirit gave the Word. He used all the gifts of the Spirit to advance the kingdom of God.

When writing gospel songs, I have prayed to God that my words and music come from God's music treasure chest of heaven. Isn't that where John Newton got the words and music to Amazing Grace? The Holy Spirit is our spiritual administrator. He is our GPS for God's way. Our success in life is measured by doing those things that please the Lord.

I believe this method could solve most of man's problems in life. Medical doctors should ask God for a word of wisdom and a word of knowledge. We need to call on the Holy Spirit for breakthroughs that will bring glory to God. He has the answer for every need.

You can imagine what a farmer's farm and harvest would be like if he didn't use all his gifts from God to grow a crop of wheat or corn. The world's first farmer scratched the ground with a stick and planted the seed. In time, he made better tools and, with God's inspiration, was able to feed nations. Today, for a higher yield at harvest time, the farmer uses his GPS to help manage the areas of the field that need more fertilizer and water. It also keeps the tractor moving on line within a specified area.

The world's first music came from a man shaking a gourd. In time, better instruments projected a better sound. Like the farmer, we now have an array of voices and instruments to make the best sound to project the message of the cross, calling sinners to repentance for salvation. The anointing of the lordship of Jesus Christ in the words and music of a believer is the only way to effectively communicate the Gospel.

The churches formed on Paul's missionary journeys were a big part of his platform for writing the Word. The Holy Spirit brought forth revelation knowledge through preaching and teaching in Paul's epistles to the churches. The word of knowledge and the word of wisdom from the Holy Spirit set up the order of the church. Paul showed the church how to use the offices in the church for the work of the ministry and for the harvest of souls for the kingdom of God.

Certainly, Paul was no different than you or me. He lived in a body that was weak, in the unknown and in constant need of spiritual repair and guidance. His body, mind and soul didn't leap into perfection the moment God called him to be an apostle. He put on the new man, which is renewed in knowledge after the image of Christ.

> "And have put on the new man, which is renewed in knowledge after the image of him that created him:" (Col. 3:10)

PRIESTS HAVE AN INFIRMITY, TOO

"For such an high priest became us, who is holy, harmless, undefiled, separate from sinners, and made higher than the heavens; Who needeth not daily, as those high priests, to offer up sacrifice, first for his own sins, and then for the people's: for this he did once, when he offered up himself. For the law maketh men **high priests which have infirmity**; but the word of the oath, which was since the law, maketh the Son, who is consecrated for evermore." (Heb. 7:26-28)

Thus by Hebrews 7:28, we find that all people have an infirmity. The flesh expresses itself in: egotism, conceit, the unknown, uncertainty and disappointment. **So, a lack of Scripture foreknowledge is a weakness of the flesh.** Therefore, abiding in the flesh is an infirmity of the flesh. It is a weakness we'll always have as long as the flesh is responding in life's state of affairs.

A Psalm of Asaph

We can begin to understand infirmity more fully if we consider what the psalmist wrote in Psalms 73. Asaph, a deep thinker, had many questions for God.

> "Truly God is good to Israel, even to such as are of a clean heart. But as for me, my feet were almost gone; my steps had well nigh slipped.
>
> "For I was envious at the foolish, when I saw the prosperity of the wicked. For there are no bands in their death: but their strength is firm. They are not in trouble as other men; neither are they plagued like other men.
>
> "Therefore pride compasseth them about as a chain; violence covereth them as a garment. Their eyes stand out with fatness: they have more than heart could wish.
>
> "They are corrupt, and speak wickedly concerning oppression: they speak loftily. They set their mouth against the heavens, and their tongue walketh through the earth.
>
> "Therefore his people return hither: and waters of a full cup are wrung out to them. And they say,

How doth God know? and is there knowledge in the most High?

"Behold, these are the ungodly, who prosper in the world; they increase in riches. Verily I have cleansed my heart in vain, and washed my hands in innocency.

"For all the day long have I been plagued, and chastened every morning. If I say, I will speak thus; behold, I should offend against the generation of thy children. When I thought to know this, it was too painful for me;" (Ps. 73:1-16)

Up to this point, we see Asaph trying to figure out why he has had to spend time keeping himself pure, being chastised by God, when he sees that the wicked are living in luxury and prosperity with apparently no penalty of sin. (Haven't we had the same thought about some popular people we see and hear throughout the world?) Then, his eyes are opened spiritually.

"Until I went into the sanctuary of God; then understood I their end. Surely thou didst set them in slippery places: thou castedst them down into destruction. How are they brought into desolation, as in a moment! they are utterly consumed with terrors.

"As a dream when one awaketh; so, O Lord, when thou awakest, thou shalt despise their image.

> **Thus my heart was grieved, and I was pricked in my reins.**
>
> "So foolish was I, and ignorant: I was as a beast before thee. Nevertheless I am continually with thee: **thou hast holden me by my right hand**. Thou shalt guide me with thy counsel, and afterward receive me to glory." Ps. 73:17-24)

Look at what Asaph discovered by going to the sanctuary of God. Many have discovered wonderful truths while in the house of God. It was there that I first heard the message of the cross. It was there that I bowed in humble thanksgiving for His mercy and forgiveness. It was there that the Lord showed me that grace and faith secured my salvation. Aren't we glad that mercy is not just one per family? Thank God for His divine restraint and patience while we learn to shed our acts of flesh by living in the law of the Spirit of life in Christ.

> "Whom have I in heaven but thee? and there is none upon earth that I desire beside thee. My flesh and my heart faileth: but God is the strength of my heart, and my portion forever.
>
> "For, lo, they that are far from thee shall perish: thou hast destroyed all them that go a whoring from thee. But it is good for me to draw near to God: I have put my trust in the Lord God, that I may declare all thy works." (Ps. 73:25-28)

What a great link to the thorn in the flesh. The Psalmist was grieved in his heart and pricked in his reins when he saw what happened to the wicked in the end. Being pricked in his reins is represented in Scripture as the seat of thoughts or affections.

The call to respond in life through the character of Christ is made clear. One glimpse of a sinner's home and destiny causes believers in Christ all over the world **to plead the sinner's case** before God day and night. Our thoughts and affections are for people to get saved!

> "I speak after the manner of men because of the **infirmity** of your flesh: for as ye have yielded your members servants to uncleanness and to iniquity unto iniquity; even so now yield your members servants to righteousness unto holiness. For when ye were the servants of sin, ye were free from righteousness." (Rom. 6:19-20)
>
> "For every high priest taken from among men is ordained for men in things pertaining to God, that he may offer both gifts and sacrifices for sins: Who can have compassion on the ignorant, and on them that are out of the way; for that **he himself also is compassed with infirmity**." (Heb. 5:1-2)
>
> "The spirit of a man will sustain his **infirmity**; but a wounded spirit who can bear?" (Prov. 18:14)

SECRETS FROM PARADISE

When Paul received his visions and revelations from paradise, the Lord warned him not to share some of its secrets. Was it not the super secret facts pertaining to the call that personalized his future position and responsibility in the Gospel? He may have been given foreknowledge of writing the letters he is now credited for in the Bible.

> "How that he was caught up into paradise, and heard **unspeakable words, which it is not lawful for a man to utter."** (2 Cor. 12:4)

How interesting to have knowledge of something super secret. God did that for Paul. What if the secret was that Paul's epistles would one day go to every nation in the world and lead millions to the saving knowledge of Jesus Christ? That is one reason why the thorn in the flesh had to be kept secret during his lifetime. It was an ecstasy unparalleled in the entire Bible.

With that in mind, it would not have been wise for him to tell Peter, James and John how the Lord was going to use him in the Gospel. What would have happened if he had said, "Do you know my epistles will be published in every language and preached all over the world?"

It would have caused unnecessary envy in the hearts of the disciples and apostles of Christ. Satan would have had a platform to accuse Paul of ego and pride.

Satan could have said, "Look at Paul, whose writings are predicted to exceed all apostles."

Satan would have whispered resentment daily to upstage the character of Christ in Paul. Satan's methods to deceive are real. Satan has been trying to cheapen and diminish the Lord from the time of Adam. It started the day he was removed from the mountain of God as profane.

It was different than when the Lord revealed some of the future to Daniel, Ezekiel and John. Paul's position in the Scriptures was to be an author of the Word as an apostle! It was a lofty, highly exalted position.

Therefore, most personal information from the Lord should remain secret. Satan takes what is spoken to undermine the Gospel. This is reason enough to be wise and keep the enemy unaware of personal motivations from God. God gives His Word to instruct, enlighten, inspire, encourage and empower believers in Christ to do works of faith.

Satan is constantly searching for some kind of indiscretion to accuse the believer of and bring down his or her testimony before God. The only way Satan is going to learn about something secret from God is through human weakness. That is why it is so important to live in the Spirit. By living in the Spirit, we are asking the Holy Spirit to guide our thoughts and affections, with full knowledge that the flesh is Satan's door of opportunity to deceive us.

> "Be sober, be vigilant; because your adversary the devil, as a roaring lion, walketh about, seeking whom he may devour:" (1 Peter 5:8)

MY UTMOST FOR HIS HIGHEST

Oswald Chambers, in My Utmost for His Highest, knew what serving God meant. He has an excellent description of being in the ministry of the Gospel of Jesus Christ. I am confident anyone could make the thorn in the flesh connection with what he wrote. I love the words of Oswald Chambers and I thank my good friend, Terry Reiff, for bringing this book of devotions to my attention. It is a very good description of the fundamental purpose of the thorn in the flesh.

•

COULD THIS BE TRUE OF ME – March 4

It is easier to serve God without a vision, easier to work for God without a call, because then you are not bothered by what God requires; common sense is your guide, veneered over with Christian sentiment. You will be more prosperous and successful, more leisure-hearted, if you never realize **the call** of God. But if once you receive a commission from Jesus Christ, the memory of what God wants will always come like a goad; you will no longer be able to work for Him on the common sense basis.

•

What a beautiful thought and devotion. The memory of the call causes Holy living; you can't do something different. Would a pastor remain in his calling? I have asked many pastors why they were a pastor. Many of them say, "Because God called me to be a pastor." None who are truly called of God will make a career change, even if a lot of money is offered. No one can do it! They know that they would be miserable trying to be a plumber, car salesman, doctor, lawyer, etc., and not obey what God called them to do.

> "For though I preach the gospel, I have nothing to glory of: for necessity is laid upon me; yea, woe is unto me, if I preach not the gospel!" (1 Cor. 9:16)

Look at Solomon, David's son. He wrote something in Ecclesiastes that is also noteworthy; it shadows the thorn in the flesh.

> "The preacher sought to find out acceptable words: and that which was written was upright, even words of truth. The words of the wise are **as goads**, and **as nails** fastened by the masters of assemblies, which are given from one shepherd." (Eccl. 12:10-11)

Well, there is only one who is wise. That one is God! The masters of assemblies were the captains under Solomon who took Solomon's orders and carried them out in directing community affairs.

You could say pastors and teachers that are preaching the Holy Word are carrying out God's orders by the Word as the Holy Spirit leads. There is only one shepherd—the Lord Jesus Christ.

> "I am the good shepherd: the good shepherd giveth his life for the sheep." (John 10:11)
>
> "For the Lord giveth wisdom : out of his mouth cometh knowledge and understanding." (Prov. 2:6)
>
> "I wisdom dwell with prudence, and find out knowledge of witty inventions." (Prov. 8:12)
>
> "That the God of our Lord Jesus Christ, the Father of glory, may give unto you the spirit of wisdom and revelation in the knowledge of him:" (Eph. 1:17)

Oh! But Paul was beginning to think that his orders from God might be in vain. He had served the Lord for seventeen years and still had nothing to prove his apostleship; though he makes that claim known by the signs and wonders that followed him.

> "Truly the signs of an apostle were wrought among you in all patience, in signs, and wonders, and mighty deeds." (2 Cor. 12:12)
>
> "Then fourteen years after I went up again to Jerusalem with Barnabas, and took Titus with me also. And I went up by revelation, and communicated unto them that gospel which I preach among the Gentiles, but privately to them which were of reputation, lest by any means I should run, or had run, in vain." (Gal. 2:1-2)

It had to wear thin on Paul, after being in full-time ministry for seventeen years, to not be recognized as an apostle. It may have shown up in a little sarcasm in his letter to the Galatians. He seemed to be directing his comments at some major players in the Gospel when he said:

> "But of these who seemed to be somewhat, (whatsoever they were, it maketh no matter to me: God accepteth no man's person:) for they who seemed to be somewhat in conference added nothing to me:" (Gal. 2:6)

WHAT THE RIGHT HANDS OF FELLOWSHIP DID

Then at the appointed time—something awesome is made known to the world. Paul is accepted as an apostle!

> "But contrariwise, when they saw that the gospel of the uncircumcision was committed unto me, as the gospel of the circumcision was unto Peter; (For he that wrought effectually in Peter to the apostleship of the circumcision, the same was mighty in me toward the Gentiles:)" (Gal. 2:7-8)

[The following Scripture is the place that proves the timeline when Paul was accepted as an apostle of Jesus Christ.]

> "And when James, Cephas, and John, who seemed to be pillars, perceived the grace that was given unto

> me, they gave to me and Barnabas the **right hands of fellowship;** that we should go unto the heathen, and they unto the circumcision. Only they would that we should remember the poor; the same which I also was forward to do." (Gal. 2:9-10)

Hallelujah! There it is! The seal to the apostleship was in the **right hands of fellowship.** Praise the Lord! Do you see what I see? Paul and Barnabas were commissioned to go to the heathen with the Gospel. Glory to God! He is now accepted as an apostle.

It has gone unknown in its true light by many of the scholars of the past. I suppose most thought Paul had always been an apostle. Then again, I don't ever remember in the last forty-some years hearing a pastor preach on Paul being rejected by the disciples (the church) in the first place. This was just not something they realized. But oh! What beautiful Scripture! What a moment in church history!

Three men known as pillars of the church—Peter, James and John—gave Paul the greatest handshake ever. It's all there in print!

The enemy was silenced for the moment. The devil would never fully recover from major heart failure. Chalk up another major victory for the Lord. Approved by the church! What a day of rejoicing. It stands out all alone—do you see it? It's unity. Oh how much it meant to Paul and his future writings to reach the world for Christ!

The right hands of fellowship given to another in church are like the hands of God. His testimony of Christ has been heard and accepted as true. His name has been recognized. He is finally accepted as one of them. It's agreeing to the same purpose. It's partnership! It speaks of one in the faith. It's an undivided force with power to influence truth. It says **welcome**.

The right hands of fellowship becomes Paul's graduation diploma—he is now linked with the other apostles. He is now recognized as in the network of the Gospel. Now you and I are one and the same. This is what Jesus prayed for concerning His disciples in John chapter 17. We have the same purpose; we are in communion and unity in Christ. Through Paul, the promotion of the glorious Gospel is spread all over the world. The time line for the right hands of fellowship is described in Acts 15:4.

> "And when they were come to Jerusalem, they were received of the **church, and of the apostles and elders**, and they declared all things that God had done with them." (Acts 15:4)

WHAT A DAY TO REJOICE IN THE LORD

My dear fellow saints, lay down the red carpet, bring out the hats and horns, blow the trumpet in Zion, let colorful balloons soar to the sky, let the doves go free. There will be dancing in the streets of Jerusalem tonight!

Well, isn't this what happens when a president is elected? I was dancing and shouting in my spirit when I found the place in Scripture where Paul was accepted by the pillars of the church as an apostle of Jesus Christ. I rejoiced! It was a historic day in Jerusalem. It should be a Christian memorial.

Paul had seventeen long years of service in the Lord so far. There was not a day that passed in the last fourteen years that he didn't wonder when he would be accepted by the church. He was battle scarred! It was an awesome victory for Paul. Praise the Lord!

He was now accepted as an apostle of Jesus Christ. Think of it! Those testimonies of the signs and wonders which followed Paul that God enabled him to do—planted the seed for Paul to be accepted as an apostle. God nudged the super apostles to take notice of Paul's teachings, preaching and his love of God. The disciples that rejected him at first finally realized that Paul was, beyond doubt, called of God.

Notice that the Scripture location for when God first confirmed Paul as an apostle of Jesus Christ is found in Acts 14:3.

> "Long time therefore abode they speaking boldly in the Lord, which gave testimony unto the word of his

grace, and **granted signs and wonders to be done by their hands."** (Acts 14:3)

Perhaps one of the obstructions hindering Paul's acceptance as an apostle is found in the statement Peter made to the disciples and the one hundred twenty, when he gave the requirement for replacing Judas:

"For it is written in the Book of Psalms, Let his habitation be desolate, and let no man dwell therein: and his bishoprick let another take. **Wherefore of these men which have companied with us all the time that the Lord Jesus went in and out among us, Beginning from the baptism of John, unto that same day that he was taken up from us, must one be ordained to be a witness with us of his resurrection.**" (Acts 1:20-22)

By these qualifications for apostleship, we can clearly see Paul did not qualify for the apostleship:

1) Paul was not companied with them all the time Jesus went in and out among them; he was not in their photo ops.
2) He was not there beginning with the baptism of John.
3) He was not one of them who witnessed the resurrection. Paul's resurrection knowledge of Jesus Christ

came on the Damascus Road. He didn't have to go to Jerusalem to look in the tomb to find him gone.

The Bible shows he was a young man when he first came on the scene in the Book of Acts—he was there witnessing the stoning of Stephen.

When Paul made his commitment to Christ, it was post-resurrection and not pre-resurrection.

> "But when it pleased God, who separated me from my mother's womb, and called me by his grace, To reveal his Son in me, that I might preach him among the heathen; immediately **I conferred not with flesh and blood: Neither went I up to Jerusalem to them which were apostles before me;** but I went into Arabia, and returned again unto Damascus." (Gal. 1:15-17)

When Stephen saw Jesus standing on the right hand of God, Jesus was already in heaven with the Father. Stephen was the first Christian martyr, and his death took place after the resurrection.

> "But he, being full of the Holy Ghost, looked up stedfastly into heaven, and saw the glory of God, and **Jesus standing on the right hand of God,** And said, Behold, I see the heavens opened, and the Son

> of man standing on the right hand of God. Then they cried out with a loud voice, and stopped their ears, and ran upon him with one accord," (Acts 7:55-57)

It appears to me that it was man that made the qualifications for the office of an apostle (bishop) by not having full knowledge or foreknowledge of God. God is the one who is sovereign, not man. Did not Paul's knowledge of Christ come by way of a vision and inspiration of the Spirit? Paul did not meet the qualification according to Peter's words, and yet, he wrote most of the New Testament.

> "For many are called, but few are chosen." (Matt. 22:14)

The gifts to man came after the resurrection of Jesus Christ and not before.

> "But unto every one of us is given grace according to the measure of the gift of Christ. Wherefore he saith, When he ascended up on high, he led captivity captive, and gave gifts unto men." (Eph. 4:7-8)

It was long after Stephen's death that Jesus appeared to Paul on the road to Damascus in a spectacular way. It was not a touch-my-nail-scarred-hands-in-the-flesh appearance. It was a vision in the spirit realm.

"And as he journeyed, he came near Damascus: and suddenly there shined round about him a **light from heaven**: And he fell to the earth, and **heard a voice** saying unto him, Saul, Saul, why persecutest thou me?

"And he said, Who art thou, Lord? And the Lord said, **I am Jesus whom thou persecutest:** it is hard for thee to kick against the pricks. And **he trembling and astonished said, Lord, what wilt thou have me to do?**

"And the Lord said unto him, Arise, and go into the city, and it shall be told thee what thou must do. And the men which journeyed with him stood speechless, hearing a voice, but seeing no man.

"And Saul arose from the earth; and when his eyes were opened, he saw no man: but they led him by the hand, and brought him into Damascus." (Acts 9:3-8)

To establish another point of reference, the appearing of Christ to Paul came long after Jesus ascended to heaven from Mount Olivet forty days after his resurrection.

"And while they looked stedfastly toward heaven as he went up, behold, two men stood by them in white apparel; Which also said, Ye men of Galilee, why stand ye gazing up into heaven? this same Jesus, which is taken up from you into heaven, shall so come in like manner as ye have seen him go into heaven." (Acts 1:10-11)

When Paul was giving his testimony to King Agrippa about meeting Christ on the Damascus road, he described how bright the light was when he was knocked to the ground.

"At midday, O king, I saw in the way a light from heaven, **above the brightness of the sun**, shining round about me and them which journeyed with me." (Acts 26:12)

Jesus is the light! We know that the natural man cannot gaze upon the sun in the sky without protective gear. Seeing Jesus in His glorified body is perhaps like glancing at the sun in the sky for just a moment. We know it's up there and feel it, but we dare not stare with wonder.

"And the city had no need of the sun, neither of the moon, to shine in it: for the glory of God did lighten it, and the Lamb is the light thereof." (Rev. 21:23)

It seems that while Paul looked upon Jesus Christ in His resurrected glorified body, the light of Christ (brighter than the sun) blinded him. Jesus is truth, and truth is also blinding to the common man. After Jesus had spoken to him, he opened his eyes, but he could not see. Yet, the words of Jesus Christ reaffirmed his call.

> "But rise, and stand upon thy feet: for I have appeared unto thee for this purpose, to make thee a minister and a witness both of these things which thou hast seen, and of those things in the which I will appear unto thee; Delivering thee from the people, and from the Gentiles, unto whom now I send thee, To open their eyes, and to turn them from darkness to light, and from the power of Satan unto God, that they may receive forgiveness of sins, and inheritance among them which are sanctified by faith that is in me." (Acts 26:16-18)

It was on the Damascus road, where Paul was brought out of darkness into the Gospel light, that he learned God had called him to the ministry.

> "Then spake Jesus again unto them, saying, I am the light of the world: he that followeth me shall not walk in darkness, but shall have the light of life." (John 8:12)
>
> "And after six days Jesus taketh Peter, James, and John his brother, and bringeth them up into an high mountain apart, And was transfigured before them:

> and his face did shine as the sun, and his raiment was white as the light." (Matt. 17:1-2)

Paul's physical eyes couldn't see natural things; but his spiritual eyes were now opened to the way, the truth and the life. The gift of faith was imparted to Paul. Seeing Christ on the Damascus road was resurrection knowledge that Jesus was alive! Ananias said that Jesus **appeared** to Paul in the way:

> "And Ananias went his way, and entered into the house; and putting his hands on him said, Brother Saul, the Lord, even Jesus, that **appeared unto thee in the way** as thou camest, hath sent me, that thou mightest receive thy sight, and be filled with the Holy Ghost." (Acts 9:17)

Salvation comes by grace through faith. Paul was saved on the road to Damascus, but filled with the Holy Ghost three days later in Damascus when Ananias put his hands on him. God used a man prequalified by God to impart the infilling of the Holy Ghost to Paul. How can anyone really know the message of the Gospel without being in Christ and empowered by the Holy Spirit? Sure we believe in Christ by faith. But you really know Jesus lives (the resurrection) when Christ is now Christ in you. You know He was raised from the dead and is present with you when you've been born again of His Spirit and filled with the Holy Ghost.

"For I delivered unto you first of all that which I also received, how that Christ died for our sins according to the Scriptures; And that he was buried, and that he rose again the third day according to the Scriptures: And that he was seen of Cephas, then of the twelve: After that, he was seen of above five hundred brethren at once; of whom the greater part remain unto this present, but some are fallen asleep. After that, he was seen of James; then of all the apostles. **And last of all he was seen of me also, as of one born out of due time.**" (1 Cor. 15:3-8)

Paul saw Christ when it was time for the Word of the Spirit to be birthed through his epistles for the Church. The Word was engraved upon his heart as he lived the Word, the Gospel of Jesus Christ. Paul was born in due time for that purpose. He was now in the rose above the thorn.

"For God, who commanded the light to shine out of darkness, hath shined in our hearts, to give the light of the knowledge of the glory of God in the face of Jesus Christ." (2 Cor. 4:6)

"Which in his times he shall shew, who is the blessed and only Potentate, the King of kings, and

> Lord of lords; Who only hath immortality, dwelling in the light which no man can approach unto; whom no man hath seen, nor can see: to whom be honour and power everlasting. Amen." (1 Tim. 6:15-16)

Moreover, when we meet Yahweh (Jesus), a change is made in us: Abram became Abraham—Jacob became Israel—and Saul became Paul, an apostle of Jesus Christ. It happens when we invite Jesus Christ into our heart and we become His temple—that's the moment of our new birth. We are born again in Christ. We are a new creature in Christ.

> "I am crucified with Christ: nevertheless I live; yet not I, but Christ liveth in me: and the life which I now live in the flesh I live by the faith of the Son of God, who loved me, and gave himself for me." (Gal. 2:20)

On that day, the old nature of Saul of Tarsus, the old man—died, and the new man, Paul, was born again in Christ. Saul was his circumcised Hebrew name that he used to study law. Paul was his Roman name that he used to write the Word to the Jews and Gentiles. The name change took place on his first missionary journey. When our old man, self, dies like Saul, we change; and in time, some become known by new names.

"And if Christ be in you, the body is dead because of sin; but the Spirit is life because of righteousness." (Rom. 8:10)

"The Spirit itself beareth witness with our spirit, that we are the children of God: And if children, then heirs; heirs of God, and joint-heirs with Christ; if so be that we suffer with him, that we may be also glorified together." (Rom. 8:16-17)

Our past life is fully known by Christ. He knows all our sins and every thought. No one can hide from an all-seeing God. His presence is divine and an awakening experience to the knowledge of truth. The Word convicts as we kneel, trembling, before Him, guilty.

"Repent ye therefore, and be converted, that your sins may be blotted out, when the times of refreshing shall come from the presence of the Lord;" (Acts 3:19)

That's why Paul, trembling and astonished, said: "Lord, what wilt thou have me to do?" He had met the Christ!

That's why he could write: "that if thou shalt confess with thy mouth the Lord Jesus, and shalt believe in thine heart that God hath raised him from the dead, thou shalt be saved." (Rom. 10:9)

The transparency of **Christ in you** is resurrection knowledge to all who have Christ in their heart. It causes us to reflect on who we are and what character we portray living the Christian life. It is humbling. We bow to God in prayer of thanksgiving, willing to share our experience of salvation to the world.

> "As ye have therefore received Christ Jesus the Lord, so walk ye in him: Rooted and built up in him, and stablished in the faith, as ye have been taught, abounding therein with thanksgiving." (Col. 2:6-7)

THE DAY I SAW CHRIST

Jesus Christ appeared to me, too. I was living near the campus of the University of Colorado in Boulder, Colorado, and studying the Holy Bible with Rudy Antle, a college student. He had asked me at church if I would like to study the Bible with him. It was just what I needed.

We met every Thursday night and studied for about an hour. He taught me to read the text of a sentence or paragraph and then pick out the key words. Then, when we met again, we would evaluate the key words that had the most meaning or application to our life. We had studied 1 Timothy and were beginning 2 Timothy. I had to look at the dictionary for meanings. I was unskilled in God's Word, but he was well informed. I still remember the Scripture that I applied to my life.

> "Let no man despise thy youth; but be thou an example of the believers, in word, in conversation, in charity, in spirit, in faith, in purity." (1 Tim. 4:12)

The study had gone on for several weeks, and then on the night before our next study, as I was taking a shower, I experienced a sacred moment of the Holy Spirit coming through the shower head with the water and cleansing me from the top of my head to the soles of my feet. In all my life, I had never felt so clean and pure. This took place about three years after I knelt at an altar and was gloriously saved. I was no longer a slave to the law of sin and death; I was being sanctified for service.

> "And such were some of you: but ye are washed, but ye are sanctified, but ye are justified in the name of the Lord Jesus, and by the Spirit of our God." (1 Cor 6:11)

During the past several weeks, I had been following the dictates of the Holy Spirit, being faithful and obedient to do the Word. I did whatever God led me to do. The very next night was the Bible study. I was sitting on my bed in a very small basement room. Rudy was sitting on a chair in front of me about four feet away. We had been sharing Bible verses with great joy when I turned and saw Jesus standing in the doorway. He was dressed in a pure white garment.

Jesus then walked in between us, stepped into Rudy, my friend, and vanished; but at the same moment He turned and came into me. I knew Jesus was in me and I was in Him. I was amazed that Christ was now in me and in my friend.

In the next day or two, as I was reading my Bible, I came across this Scripture in 2 Cor. 5:17:

> "Therefore if any man be **in Christ**, he is a new creature: old things are passed away; behold, all things are become new." (2 Cor. 5:17)

The Word of God came alive to me. Jesus Christ in me! I was in Christ. He quickened my total being. I, too, was now a living witness to the resurrection of Jesus Christ. I had proof that Christ was alive. Christ was in me! I changed. The next day, and many days that followed, I wondered if people could see Jesus in me. Then I found more Scripture that riveted my soul.

> "Abide in me, and I in you. As the branch cannot bear fruit of itself, except it abide in the vine; no more can ye, except ye abide in me. I am the vine, ye are the branches: He that abideth in me, and I in him, the same bringeth forth much fruit: for without me ye can do nothing." (John 15:4-5)

We are set apart for God's use. It's being in Christ that positions us to escape condemnation and judgment. It puts us in the vine to bear fruit. It's walking in the Word, in Christ. It's the ultimate position for a believer that is confirmed in the Lord's Prayer: Thy Kingdom come Thy will be done on earth as it is in heaven. Living in Christ is glorifying our Heavenly Father!

> "But know that the Lord hath set apart him that is godly for himself: the Lord will hear when I call unto him. Stand in awe, and sin not: commune with your own heart upon your bed, and be still. Selah. Offer the sacrifices of righteousness, and put your trust in the Lord." (Ps. 4:3-5)

Behold! The words in Christ appear in the Bible seventy-seven times, and seventy-five of the words in Christ are referenced by Paul; the other two by Peter. Being in Christ and not in the flesh is the position of sanctification and righteousness.

> "For in him dwelleth all the fulness of the Godhead bodily. And ye are complete in him, which is the head of all principality and power:" (Col. 2:9-10)

Jesus was not a historical Jesus to me from that day forward. He was Jesus in me—the hope of glory. I went to work with the Word living in me. I walked around other people with Christ in me and me in Him. I knew the light of Christ would now shine out of me.

Thereafter, I began to look for people who also appeared to have Jesus living in them. Some of these dear saints lived the life of Christ in all they did. My mother, Helen Berg, lived in Christ. I never saw Mom's sin nature except maybe once. It was when I made her upset by something I did and she said, "Darn you!" I was shocked because Mom truly lived the cross.

I was telling this to Mary, my wife, and she said I evidently needed repairing, because darn is what mothers do to mend their children's socks. Well, mom did the repair; she broke off a tree branch and added some blisters to my backside! My aunt Ines Berg lived in Christ too. I often asked my aunt to remember me in her prayers. I know she did.

After about twenty years had passed, I saw a man who had gone to that same church where I first met Rudy. I asked him if he knew whatever happened to Rudy. He didn't. But later that night he called me, said he did some checking, and found he was now a pastor at a Baptist church in Aurora, Colorado.

Amazingly, he only lived about twenty miles from me. So I decided I would go meet him; I went to his church on a Wednesday night, and after the service we got together for fellowship. I asked him if he remembered Jesus walking in on our Bible study. He said that he remembered a moment when I mentioned that I had seen Jesus Christ, but he didn't see Him.

I wondered why. Now, after years, I think I know why Rudy didn't see what I saw. Rudy was very intelligent. He had read and studied the Bible from his youth. He had the revelation and manifestation of Christ from reading the Word, and by faith, he was trusting in Christ.

But I was unlearned and needed special education. This was my first Bible study. I believe one of the reasons Jesus appeared to me was because of the depth of my call for help. I had been crying out to God. I was solemnly seeking Him with all of my heart, mind and soul.

When this happened it really strengthened my faith. But ultimately, I was being prepared to serve the Lord, for God had an assignment for me. You only need to see Jesus Christ once and the manifestation of Christ will change your life forever. I suppose I needed to catch up quickly for what God had planned for me to do.

In time I became a distributor of Christian books and Bibles to Bible book stores and supermarkets in many of our western States. In over twenty years, I screened thousands of books for distribution.

When Jesus Christ stepped into Rudy's life and came into mine at the same moment, that was His divine nature. It revealed His omnipresence. God, in a single moment, opened my mind and heart to understand the Word. I knew Christ was in me, and the Word backed up what had happened. It gave me volumes of Scriptural knowledge, the wisdom of Christ and understanding. The Word was living in me.

I'm forever grateful and thankful to Rudy Antle for being obedient to the Lord by inviting me to study the Bible with him. He gave me confidence that I could learn the Word and he showed me how to study the Word. Thank you Rudy!

THE APPEARING CHRIST IS RESURRECTION KNOWLEDGE

Paul's writings were not historical in nature; he didn't give a historical account of Christ. He wrote about God from the point of creation as Creator. He revealed Christ through his own life by the inspiration of the Holy Spirit. When Paul wrote the words in Christ as Scripture text, he was **in** Christ. He was a prisoner of Christ. He was revealing the message from God to the church.

> "For the invisible things of him from the creation of the world are clearly seen, being understood by the things that are made, even his eternal power and Godhead; so that they are without excuse:" (Rom 1:20)

Paul did not know Jesus in the flesh like Peter, James and John. Thus, when Jesus appeared to Paul, on the road to Damascus, the presence of Christ gave him resurrection knowledge. The resurrection knowledge of Jesus Christ became real as Jesus took up residence in Paul's heart.

What a tremendous day! The apostleship was his position in the faith, and it came to Paul by revelation of God; however, it was not approved by the church until the disciples, through the gift of discernment, saw and heard of the signs and wonders God had worked through Paul.

That approval of Paul's apostleship was the greatest handshake the world has ever known. It unified the church. It strengthened and encouraged Paul. It brought out brotherly love from within the church. It showed that we can accomplish mighty works of God when we agree as believers and are in union with Christ.

This is one of the highest forms of recognition given, and rarely do we see a pastor using it to bring unity to the ministry by telling the congregation to give the one next to you the right hands of fellowship. It would be a godly moment of honor if our leaders would use this expression when someone is joining the church or ordaining leaders of the church.

> "Behold, how good and how pleasant it is for brethren to dwell together in unity! It is like the precious ointment upon the head, that ran down upon the beard,

> even Aaron's beard: that went down to the skirts of his garments; As the dew of Hermon, and as the dew that descended upon the mountains of Zion: for there the LORD commanded the blessing, even life for evermore." (Ps. 133:1-3)

When he wrote in Galatians 2:9 the words, those who seemed to be pillars—they were the pillar-apostles. The right hands-shake was the seal to the apostleship. All glory to God! He didn't say right hand, as one, but right hands signifying they all agreed. It was a majority vote. Where was his accuser now? The accuser—Satan—and his lying messenger went dumb, unable to speak, disarmed by the right hands of fellowship.

It took many years to receive it—to see the day of graduation—but now Paul's labor in the Lord was not in vain. Also, his writings were approved by the church. Today, millions have copies of Paul's writings.

You would think that a seven-day celebration feast would be in order, as this was one of the greatest events in Bible history.

After writing about the right hands of fellowship, Paul mentioned that he confronted Peter about resorting back to the works of the law of sin and death and avoiding the message of **the cross, which is the law of the Spirit of the life in Christ**.

"But when Peter was come to Antioch, I withstood him to the face, because he was to be blamed. For before that certain came from James, he did eat with the Gentiles: but when they were come, he withdrew and separated himself, fearing them which were of the circumcision.

"And the other Jews dissembled likewise with him; insomuch that Barnabas also was carried away with their dissimulation. But when I saw that they walked not uprightly according to the truth of the gospel, I said unto Peter before them all, If thou, being a Jew, livest after the manner of Gentiles, and not as do the Jews, why compellest thou the Gentiles to live as do the Jews?" (Gal. 2:11-14)

In Antioch, Peter's behavior was not in true character of the Gospel the Word makes its appeal for; therefore, Paul corrected Peter in front of them all. Peter talked and ate like the cross had set him free from the law of sin and death (sin nature) until the Jews entered the room, then he returned to the Jewish-wall of saved by circumcision that separated the Jews from the Greeks. But the law of circumcision had no power to change a person's life. This wall had been brought down by Paul's writings about the cross—that salvation is by grace through faith and **not of works of some law**—yet some were foolishly working to rebuild the wall.

"And I, brethren, if I yet preach circumcision, why do I yet suffer persecution? then is the offence of the cross ceased." (Gal 5:11)

Preaching the law of circumcision will not offend anyone or save anyone. Only the cross offends and leads the sinner to salvation by grace through faith. If the cross is not preached to offend, there is no salvation!

The life to live in Christ is not self-made and not of self-works of following the law. It is being cross-conscious and Christ-conscious that your life is now Christ living in you, and you living in Christ. Paul's confrontation with Peter shows us why it was so necessary that Peter be corrected. Paul knew in Christ we are free from the condemnation of the law of circumcision (the law of sin and death was nailed to the tree). In Christ there is no law to condemn us. In light of this, some of the greatest words ever penned come from Peter.

"If any man speak, let him speak as the oracles of God; if any man minister, let him do it as of the ability which God giveth: that God in all things may be glorified through Jesus Christ, to whom be praise and **dominion** for ever and ever. Amen." (1 Peter 4:11)

It shows that Paul had great influence in the Apostle Peter's life and character by what Peter wrote in his epistles concerning Paul.

> "Nevertheless we, according to his promise, look for new heavens and a new earth, wherein dwelleth righteousness. Wherefore, beloved, seeing that ye look for such things, be diligent that ye may be found of him in peace, without spot, and blameless.
>
> "And account that the longsuffering of our Lord is salvation; even as our beloved brother Paul also according to the wisdom given unto him hath written unto you; As also in all his epistles, speaking in them of these things; in which are some things hard to be understood, which they that are unlearned and unstable wrest, as they do also the other Scriptures, unto their own destruction." (2 Peter 3:13-16)

I am sure Peter and Paul had great fellowship discussing the dominion we have in Christ. Paul may have even asked about the time Jesus took Peter, James and John on a high mountain and was transfigured, and there appeared Moses and Elias. It was our future new body on display.

> "That which we have seen and heard declare we unto you, that ye also may have fellowship with us: and

truly our fellowship is with the Father, and with his Son Jesus Christ." (1 John 1:3)

The one who introduces us to Christ is the Holy Spirit. Then Jesus shows us the Father. Jesus is the one who gives us the right hands of fellowship. Thus, living in Christ we have fellowship with the Father.

"Neither is there salvation in any other: for there is none other name under heaven given among men, whereby we must be saved." (Acts 4:12)

No one can give an excuse for not understanding what the Scriptures say. For the Lord fulfilled His promise to send another Comforter to guide in all truth. Many have given amazing testimonies that they have received spiritual assistance in just the right moment from the Holy Spirit. Many have asked for power to serve, personal guidance, wisdom, knowledge and understanding from the Comforter.

However, some shy away from acknowledging the Holy Spirit in their lives. He is left out of their petition when prayer is made. He seems to be absent from many churches. But the Scriptures show that He is our Comforter and special guide while seeking God's will in any matter.

"And I will pray the Father, and he shall give you another Comforter, that he may abide with you

> forever; Even the Spirit of truth; whom the world cannot receive, because it seeth him not, neither knoweth him: but ye know him; for he dwelleth with you, and shall be in you. I will not leave you comfortless: I will come to you." (John 14:16-18)

None of these connections of truth that I am making in this book could be made without the Holy Spirit guiding me. He said He would abide, and He does. He said He is the **Spirit of truth,** and He is. He said I shall know Him, and I do. He said the Comforter will not leave me comfortless, and I have that comfort and assurance. Comfort is following the dictates of the Holy Spirit.

In 1 Thessalonians 5:19-21 it says: "quench not the Spirit: despise not prophesying; prove all things; hold fast that which is good."

One day my whole world fell apart. I thought the Lord had abandoned me. My journey with God had taken me into deep waters of the unknown. It was the darkest night of my life—it was like what happened to John the Baptist when he was in prison and about to lose his head. He sent two of his disciples to ask Jesus, "art thou he that should come, or do we look for another?" His faith was on empty, and he needed a refilling of truth and vision. He was living out of his fear instead of **by faith**. So he stopped and asked for directions.

"Jesus answered and said unto them, Go and shew John again those things which ye do hear and see: The blind receive their sight, and the lame walk, the lepers are cleansed, and the deaf hear, the dead are raised up, and the poor have the gospel preached to them. And blessed is he, whosoever shall not be offended in me." (Matt. 11:4-6)

By the Lord's help, I had built a massive sales program that needed dividing and supervision. I had put every ounce of my being into creating sales. I even arranged the product by content and color on the displays to enhance sales. I was on the cutting edge of performance. I thought the company would recognize my success, but they remained silent. I soon realized the sales manager had left me alone to fail because I had witnessed to him that Christ was the way. Pressure to maintain the excellence of sales had become unbearable. It was now a force too large to maintain without help. Defeat was closing in on me. I fell to my knees in prayer. I cried out to God! After my words were exhausted, all I could do in prayer was groan. I was groaning in the Spirit.

"Likewise the Spirit also helpeth our infirmities: for we know not what we should pray for as we ought: but the Spirit itself maketh intercession for us with groanings which cannot be uttered." (Rom. 8:26)

While I was still on my knees praying, it seemed I was losing grip on the purpose of life itself. I searched for faith in all the people I knew that had given testimony of faith in God. Many of them were saints in the church; but as I studied their lives, none of them seemed to have enough faith for what I needed. Then when all the light of hope had faded away and darkness was too dark to see, God showed me a vision of Jesus on the road to Calvary and Jesus Christ on the cross. It was as real as though I was there the day when they nailed Jesus to the tree. I was looking at the author of faith before I read about Him in Hebrews 12:1-2. His act of faith was total and complete. It gave me hope and peace. Oh, how many times after that day have I looked at what Jesus did on the cross to recharge my faith.

All glory to the Lord! I found joy in the morning. God responded to my prayers with a word of wisdom that took the burden and yoke off my shoulders and gave me perfect rest. He gave me a way to escape so that I could bear the unknown.

At my workplace, I had taken on hours of extra work that wasn't part of my job description. I wasn't getting paid for it, either. When I finished my normal work, I'd return to the same stores later in the evening on my own time and write down items of merchandise that had sold out. Then I refilled the shelves the next day with the items that the log-forms couldn't keep up with. It was before barcodes came on the scene and enabled computer control for thousands of items in supermarkets and stores. God gifted me to accurately predict the stores' needs, and it increased sales by thousands of dollars. I'd been doing this for over a year and sales were phenomenal.

Here is how I escaped: in the morning at a supermarket, my burden was more than I could bear. I nearly collapsed from exhaustion. I was organizing displays and handling books and magazines; all items seemingly weighed more than I could lift. In the struggle and certain defeat—softly, the Holy Spirit gave me a word of wisdom (something to know and do). I was instructed to go to the company owners and apologize for taking this responsibility on myself and to release it back to their control. Hallelujah! Faith refreshed my heart. Joy and peace came flooding over my body and the mountain was removed.

My burden was gone, and the pressure of trying to figure out how to control all the merchandise and sales vanished. Thus, I went to the company and told them I was sorry for taking all of these extra responsibilities upon myself. They were glad to hear that I was yielding it to their control.

God was doing something in all of this, so I patiently waited to see what was going to happen next. It cost the company unknown thousands of dollars of lost sales over the next several months; yet, the sales manager was so power hungry for full control of all areas of the company (he was part owner) that he seemed willing to take the loss for more control.

Later, realizing his loss of revenue and the fact that he had been outwitted, he attempted to brainwash me. I suddenly realized that this is not my battle, but the Lord's. I was not the one who outwitted him; it was the Lord. The Holy Spirit was the one who gave me the word of wisdom that I spoke at the appointed time. I write more about this in the chapter, "Secret Knowledge and Wisdom through the Call of God."

> "And he said, Hearken ye, all Judah, and ye inhabitants of Jerusalem, and thou king Jehoshaphat, Thus saith the LORD unto you, Be not afraid nor dismayed by reason of this great multitude; for the battle is not yours, but God's." (2 Chron. 20:15)

I had sweet peace, wonderful peace, knowing that the Lord was fighting my battle. I was reading the Bible daily and listening to my pastor's historical messages about the Bible; but this was not history. I was living in Christ and following the dictates of the Holy Ghost. It was real time!

In all my contacts with company management and owners, I was well aware of how Christ was presented through me to them. I lived as Christ to them. I loved them as Christ loved them. I managed my time as a faithful servant. After several months of lost sales, I told the owners that the Lord was now leading me to rebuild their revenues higher than ever before. Well, they soon had to divide the company to handle the volume of business. God had anointed me for their success.

> "And if ye have not been faithful in that which is another man's, who shall give you that which is your own?" (Luke 16:12)

Therefore, trusting in the Holy Spirit lifted me out of the self-conscious mode and put me into the Spirit-conscious mode. I prayed to God (our Heavenly Father) through Christ living in me, and the Holy Spirit guided me into the next discovery the Lord had planned for my life. The unknowns became known and Christ was glorified day by day as I experienced a cross-consciousness in my daily activities.

It is through prayer and the Holy Spirit that our eyes are opened to see what the Lord is doing or going to do through Christ in us. The Holy Ghost is our personal contractor that helps us build our house of faith. In Jude 20 it says: "but ye, beloved, building up yourselves on your most holy faith, praying in the Holy Ghost."

Paul wrote that we should pray without ceasing. It is essential to our walk in Christ as we build up ourselves in the holy faith. I was living in the faith zone and praying continually. To please our heavenly Father, we must be Christ-conscious, cross-conscious, and Holy Ghost-conscious.

"And Enoch also, the seventh from Adam, prophesied of these, saying, Behold, the Lord cometh with ten thousands of his saints, To execute judgment upon all, and to convince all that are ungodly among them of all their ungodly deeds which they have ungodly committed, and of all their hard speeches which ungodly sinners have spoken against him.

"These are murmurers, complainers, walking after their own lusts; and their mouth speaketh great swelling words, having men's persons in admiration because of advantage. But, beloved, remember ye the words which were spoken before of the apostles of our Lord Jesus Christ; How that they told you there should be mockers in the last time, who should walk after their own ungodly lusts.

"These be they who separate themselves, sensual, having not the Spirit. **But ye, beloved, building up yourselves on your most holy faith, praying in the Holy Ghost**, Keep your selves in the love of God, looking for the mercy of our Lord Jesus Christ unto eternal life.

"And of some have compassion, **making a difference**: And others save with fear, pulling them out of the fire; hating even the garment spotted by the flesh. Now unto him that is able to keep you from falling, and to present you faultless before the presence of his glory with exceeding joy, To the only wise God our

Saviour, be glory and majesty, dominion and power, both now and ever. Amen." (Jude 14-25)

Paul was making a difference in the world and trusted God; yet, he had to win over those pillar-apostles by the miracles of God—the signs and wonders; because, as we have previously shown, he did not meet the qualifications Peter listed.

"I am become a fool in glorying; ye have compelled me: for I ought to have been commended of you: for in nothing am I behind the very chiefest apostles, though I be nothing." (2 Cor. 12:11)

The only references to this office in Psalms mentioned in Acts 1:20 are as follows:

"Let their habitation be desolate; and let none dwell in their tents." (Ps. 69:25)

"When he shall be judged, let him be condemned: and let his prayer become sin. Let his days be few; and **let another take his office**." (Ps. 109:7-8)

However, Peter's ruling makes perfect theological New Testament sense, showing the foundational truth of the Gospel. For all who hold an office of the church must know the purpose of the baptism of John, the teachings of Christ and the cross and the resurrection of Jesus Christ. There are three major components of the Gospel that must be fully revealed and understood by a disciple or an apostle of Christ:

1. Christ in you is the hope of glory. "To whom God would make known what is the riches of the glory of this mystery among the Gentiles; which is Christ in you, the hope of glory:" (Col. 1:27)
2. Water baptism: the sign the new believer is following in obedience to Christ, in His death, and in His resurrection. "For if we have been planted together in the likeness of his death, we shall be also in the likeness of his resurrection: Knowing this, that our old man is crucified with him, that the body of sin might be destroyed, that henceforth we should not serve sin." (Rom. 6:5-6)
3. Belief in the cross and the resurrection is a prerequisite to salvation. In essence, one must believe in Jesus Christ, His death on the cross, and His resurrection to be saved. "That if thou shalt confess with thy mouth the Lord Jesus, and shalt believe in thine heart that God hath raised him from the dead, thou shalt be saved." (Rom. 10:9)

When the ruling was made, Peter was with the disciples and the one hundred twenty waiting for the Holy Ghost. He may have been impatient—he was known to take action quickly. He did cut off a man's ear in the Garden of Gethsemane in the presence of Jesus. It could easily be debated that he got ahead of God by naming another bishop at that point. However, the other disciples agreed with him to select another.

In the ensuing days Matthias was selected when the disciples cast lots, but he is never mentioned again.

Did Peter forge ahead of God, before the Lord called Paul to be an apostle, out of due time?

Still, most of Peter's statement has deep scriptural truth and is essential to the Gospel. For it is imperative that a leader teaching or preaching the Gospel of Jesus Christ know the fundamentals of the faith. How could anyone be a bishop and not be **in Christ** or know 'Jesus' and his teachings?

We hear some preach a bishop is not for today; but why did Paul show the qualifications for the office of a **bishop,** if Matthias or Paul were the last bishops? Paul, who was disqualified by Peter's words, is the one to set church order for holding a high office.

> "A bishop then must be blameless, the husband of one wife, vigilant, sober, of good behaviour, given to hospitality, apt to teach; Not given to wine, no striker, not greedy of filthy lucre; but patient, not a brawler, not covetous; One that ruleth well his own house,

having his children in subjection with all gravity; (For if a man know not how to rule his own house, how shall he take care of the church of God?) Not a novice, lest being lifted up with pride he fall into the condemnation of the devil." (1 Tim. 3:2-6)

Paul wrote that Jesus gave gifts unto men. God's plan and purpose of these gifts by members of the body of Christ were for **unity** and **perfection** of the church. What is clear here is that the objective of the officers and offices of the church **is for perfecting the saints**.

"Wherefore he saith, When he ascended up on high, he led captivity captive, and gave gifts unto men. (Now that he ascended, what is it but that he also descended first into the lower parts of the earth? He that descended is the same also that ascended up far above all heavens, that he might fill all things.)

"And he gave some, apostles; and some, prophets; and some, evangelists; and some, pastors and teachers; For the perfecting of the saints, for the work of the ministry, for the edifying of the body of Christ:

"Till we all come in the unity of the faith, and of the knowledge of the Son of God, unto a perfect man, unto the measure of the stature of the fullness of Christ:" (Eph. 4:8-13)

All the officers of the offices hold sanctified distinction that is separate from the ordinary. They are for holy service to the Lord; they are intended for three purposes and four goals to accomplish.

THREE PURPOSES FOR THE FIVE OFFICES

1. For the perfecting of the saints.
2. For the work of the ministry.
3. For the edifying of the body of Christ.

FOUR MAJOR GOALS TO ACCOMPLISH

1. **Until all come** in the unity of the faith.
2. **Until all come** to the knowledge of the Son of God.
3. **Until all come** to be a perfected in Christ.
4. **Until all come** unto the measure of the stature of the fullness of Christ.

There are many at work in the ministry, but when have **all come** to the unity of the faith? When have we **all come** to the knowledge of the Son of God? When have we **all come** to be perfected in Christ? When have **all come** <u>unto the measure of the stature of the fullness of Christ</u>?

<u>"That we henceforth be no more children, tossed to and fro, and carried about with every wind of doctrine, by</u>

the sleight of men, and cunning craftiness, whereby they lie in wait to deceive; But speaking the truth in love, may grow up into him in all things, which is the head, even Christ:" (Eph. 4:14-15)

The case made here is that apostles, prophets, evangelists, pastors and teachers are all needed to work together to fulfill the goals of the ministry of the Gospel: **until all come to the four goals listed above**.

In Church history, our leaders have taken stands on issues that have caused church splits, strife and division. Was love abandoned with these issues? Are church leaders enforcing man's ideas in music and programs as law (of the sin nature) in having authority over the law of the Spirit of life in Christ? Is not the Holy Spirit restricted (quenched) in this kind of church? A legalist (of the law of sin and death) is spiritually blind to many of the workings of the Holy Spirit. The reason is the Holy Spirit doesn't work through the law.

Much of what we hear and see in churches today comes from **grace space** (the grace God gives those of faith, when what is done is in the weakness of the law). But Oh! What an impact the Gospel makes when the Holy Spirit has been personally invited to be in control, when we come together to do the Lord's business, break bread or to worship Christ.

Are we as a church becoming more stand-alone or independent, being more apart with differences and disagreements than being in unity? Is not 1 Cor. 13:7 still true that love **<u>believes all things</u>** instead of disagreeing with most everyone? Where are examples of churches in agreement abounding in love?

LEST ANY MAN SHOULD THINK OF ME

There are great statements in the Bible. John the Baptist made perhaps two of the greatest statements when he looked upon Jesus Christ and said, "Behold the Lamb of God which takes away the sin of the world" and "He must increase, but I must decrease."

Paul did so, too, when he said, "Lest any man think of me above that which he sees me to be or hears of me."

Every believer should contemplate this every day. It should be our goal of the day—to be sensitive to the Word while being aware of his or her character so that no one sees or hears anything out of the character of Jesus Christ, our Lord. Yet, the only way possible to keep our character humble in Christ is the Word, or like Paul, **the call** of God. **The call is our compass** that keeps pointing to Christ.

The thorn in the flesh will last as long as we are living on earth. **The call** requires the highest standard of living that is available to live in Christ. **The call** is to live in the message of the cross. By being available, God will do mighty things in you and through you. The Lord is calling you today. If you read the Word, obey it and listen; you will hear Him call. If you feel in any way disconnected with God or He does not reveal Christ to you do this:

> "He that hath my commandments, and keepeth them, he it is that loveth me: and he that loveth me shall be loved of my Father, and I will love him, **and will manifest myself to him**." (John 14:21)

Walking in obedience to **the call** is what keeps our lives free from the guilt of sin. **The call** is our navigator through life. It shows the position in which to serve Christ. **The call** pleads for Holy living so that we are safe from condemnation. **The call** came from the Word, and the Word was the thorn that caused the flesh to yield to the way of the Spirit.

FAMILIARITY

Familiarity with the Bible or a person attracts an open arm approach in the choice of words we speak and what we do, with liberty and freedom. Yet, **the call** of God points us to the character of Christ in all we say and do. For instance, a boy that is using all of his charm and wit to win his girl friend's heart, will not take liberty in using just any kind of words or practice bad conduct in her company, for fear of her giving him the cold-shoulder.

However, once they are married, familiarity can open doors to careless liberty in their behavior. If someone's behavior, in regards to manners and words, is no longer carefully chosen by what Christ would say and do, it can cause unhealthy wounds in their relationship. If these things are not forgiven, hurt settles in the heart and causes hardness of the heart. This is why Moses **suffered** to write for some people a bill of divorcement. **The call** helped Paul live <u>in the character of an apostle</u> at all times, regardless of the liberty and freedom he had won with familiarity with someone.

To stay in the call, Paul had to live in the Spirit absent of the flesh. **The call** made Paul a supple person, soft and compliant, to the voice of the Holy Spirit. Jesus Christ was Lord of his life. It was the Lordship of Jesus Christ which brought the anointing.

The word supple is found only once in the Bible, and it pertained to the birth of Jerusalem.

> <u>"And as for thy nativity, in the day thou wast born thy navel was not cut, neither wast thou washed in water to supple thee; thou wast not salted at all, nor swaddled at all." (Ezek. 16:4)</u>

Webster says supple means to be compliant; soft; readily adaptable or responsive to new situations; to perform bending or twisting movements with ease; capable of bending or folding without creases, cracks or breaking.

The softness of a baby in the hands of love is the picture here. It is saying to train up a child in the way he should go and when he is old, he will not depart from it. A child can bend, twist, and flex the joints, muscles, tongue, heart and mind to have faith in God's Word, through training, when young. A child can easily form good habits. He learns quicker and is more useful to the Lord sooner and longer.

Paul's heart was supple to the Word. His character was supple to the measure of the call. His voice was supple toward others as he preached the Word to save the lost. His soft voice caused them to want to hear more and join His purpose and mission.

The thorn in the flesh, **the call**, disciplined Paul to be supple. The call did it! The call was like a school master. It made his heart soft. The call caused lasting obedience as an apostle, anointed by the oil of the Holy Spirit, being supple, showing the character of Jesus Christ.

It causes us to think of the chastisement of God. Chastisement comes for our good. God knows our frame and what it takes to bear the peaceable fruit of righteousness.

> "For whom the Lord loveth he chasteneth, and scourgeth every son whom he receiveth. If ye endure chastening, God dealeth with you as with sons; for what

son is he whom the father chasteneth not?" ((Heb. 12:6-7)

"For they verily for a few days chastened us after their own pleasure; but he for our profit, that we might be partakers of his holiness. Now no chastening for the present seemeth to be joyous, but grievous: nevertheless afterward it yieldeth the peaceable fruit of righteousness unto them which are exercised thereby." (Heb. 12:10-11)

The opposite of supple, in Bible terms, would be people that are stiff-necked, in unbelief and have an uncircumcised heart. People that are in rebellion and resist the commandments of God have a hard heart and are noncompliant to the supple touch of the Lord. This kind of heart is not sensitive to the dictates of the Holy Spirit, to be guided by the Word, as an example of Christ to others, in what they say or do.

"Ye stiffnecked and uncircumcised in heart and ears, ye do always resist the Holy Ghost: as your fathers did, so do ye." (Acts 7:51)

"For rebellion is as the sin of witchcraft, and stubbornness is as iniquity and idolatry. Because thou hast rejected the word of the Lord, he hath also rejected thee from being king." (1 Sam. 15:23)

"Take this book of the law, and put it in the side of the ark of the covenant of the Lord your God, that it may be there for a witness against thee. For I know thy rebellion, and thy stiff neck: behold, while I am yet alive with you this day, ye have been rebellious against the Lord; and how much more after my death?" (Deut. 31:26-27)

"He openeth also their ear to discipline, and commandeth that they return from iniquity. If they obey and serve him, they shall spend their days in prosperity, and their years in pleasures. But if they obey not, they shall perish by the sword, and they shall die without knowledge." (Job 36:10-12)

A good example in today's use of supple is: a cowboy rubs oil into the leather of his saddle to make it supple—soft. If we will be like Paul and follow after Christ, we will be supple. The secret is obeying, submitting and yielding to the Word as you read it.

On RDF TV, I saw a cowboy do some amazing things with a wild horse that had never been touched or ridden by man. He approached the horse with gentleness. He talked softly to the horse. He rubbed the horse in all the right spots. He made himself friendly. He did a variety of things to cause the horse to want to join up with him.

Within thirty minutes the cowboy was riding the horse around the arena. When the cowboy dismounted and started walking away slowly—the horse followed. The horse wanted more of what was supple, soft and gentle. He willingly accepted the cowboy and his training. The horse felt no danger! The cowboy gave the horse gentle care and love. He had found a friend.

> "Ho, every one that thirsteth, come ye to the waters, and he that hath no money; come ye, buy, and eat; yea, come, buy wine and milk without money and without price. Wherefore do ye spend money for that which is not bread? and your labour for that which satisfieth not? hearken diligently unto me, and eat ye that which is good, and let your soul delight itself in fatness.
>
> "Incline your ear, and come unto me: hear, and your soul shall live; and I will make an everlasting covenant with you, even the sure mercies of David." (Isa. 55:1-3)
>
> "Seek ye the Lord while he may be found, call ye upon him while he is near: Let the wicked forsake his way, and the unrighteous man his thoughts: and let him return unto the Lord, and he will have mercy upon him; and to our God, for he will abundantly pardon.
>
> "For my thoughts are not your thoughts, neither are your ways my ways, saith the Lord. For as the heavens are higher than the earth, so are my ways higher than your ways, and my thoughts than your thoughts." (Isa. 55:6-9)

IN THE BEGINNING THERE WERE FIVE PARTS TO THE THORN

At first, there were five parts to Paul's thorn in the flesh:

1) The call of God to be an apostle of Jesus Christ; but God didn't tell the other apostles what He had done.
2) The rejection Paul got from the disciples and the church, when he came to Jerusalem to join the team.
3) The vow or announcement Paul made to the followers of Christ that he was an apostle of Jesus Christ. He did so at the beginning of his ministry, and yet it took a total of seventeen years of ministry before he was accepted as an apostle by the pillars of the church.
4) The messenger of Satan buffeting him, accusing him of not being an apostle.

5) When Peter, James and John, the pillars of the church, did not recognize Paul as an apostle.

"And he said unto me, My grace is sufficient for thee: for my strength is made perfect in weakness. Most gladly therefore will I rather glory in my infirmities, that the power of Christ may rest upon me. Therefore I take **pleasure in infirmities**, in reproaches, in necessities, in persecutions, in distresses for Christ's sake: for when I am weak, then am I strong. I am become a fool in glorying; ye have compelled me: for I ought to have been commended of you: for in nothing am I behind the very chiefest apostles, though I be nothing." (2 Cor. 12:9-11)

The Holy Bible comes alive when you see a mystery like Paul's thorn in the flesh revealed before your eyes. When we look at all five parts to the thorn in the flesh, each one did something to cause Paul to be supple and live holy before God.

We see God's message of grace was extended to Paul, and that Paul, by faith, worked through infirmities: the unknowns, egotism, and weakness. He overcame the unknowns for the sake of Christ.

"Then said the Lord unto me, Thou hast well seen: for I will hasten my word to perform it." (Jer. 1:12)

ONLY ONE OF THE FIVE PARTS OF THE THORN REMAINED

When Paul received the right hands of fellowship, only one part of the thorn in the flesh remained. The **first** part of the thorn in the flesh, <u>the call</u> of God, will always remain to prick the flesh to live in the character of Christ—as long as the natural flesh (sin nature) is a part of us while on earth. Yet, while living in Christ, we are exempt from the pricking of the Word. When we are consciously living in obedience to the Word and the dictates of the Holy Spirit, the law of sin and death is silenced. The law of the Spirit of life in Christ has dominion (supreme authority) over our sin nature and the will to sin—the law of sin and death (Romans chapter seven). The Law of Moses came to show me what I once was, but the law of the Spirit of life in Christ came to show me who I am now. There is nothing greater than living in the rose above the thorn (Romans chapter eight). Our thoughts are focused on what Jesus did at the cross, as we walk in victory of the cross. We are free! It feels good to be in Christ. Think Christ!

The **second** part of the thorn in the flesh, the rejection he got from the disciples of Christ, the church, became a thing of the past after he was accepted by the brotherly seal of the right hands of fellowship.

The **third** part of the thorn in the flesh, the vow, the announcement that Paul made to the followers of Christ, was fulfilled when he was given the right hands of fellowship.

The **fourth** part of the thorn in the flesh, the messenger of Satan buffeting him about not being an apostle, became a thing of the past when Paul received the right hands of fellowship from Peter, James and John. He also overcame Satan by reminding him of the victory in Jesus Christ for all believers that was won at Calvary, by His redeeming Blood and the resurrection of Christ. We know the devil trembles at that name—**JESUS.**

The **fifth** part of the thorn in the flesh, the apostles Peter, James and John, would be the ones to make the apostleship possible. It happened when they gave Paul the right hands of fellowship. Behold! It was fulfilled.

Now, all the parts of Paul's thorn in the flesh were either fulfilled or done away with but one. The only one remaining was **the call. The call** remained to remind Paul that he was to live in Christ, in the Word, as long as his time on earth remained. The thorn in the flesh remained with Paul until Jesus called him home.

SECRET KNOWLEDGE AND WISDOM THROUGH THE CALL OF GOD

It was early in the morning when I left Guymon, Oklahoma, my hometown, returning to beautiful Colorado after making restitution for my youth. When I reached Dalhart, Texas, I picked up a hitch-hiker going my way. He had a few personal belongings in a bag and said he was going to Trinidad, Colorado.

Out on the highway I began telling him what Jesus Christ was doing in my life—how He forgave me of my sin and made me a new creation in Him. I wanted to share the good news with the whole world. When we got to Trinidad, I took him to a restaurant and bought him a steak dinner, then I gave him all the money I had. I remember thinking I had a job in Boulder, and he seemed to have nothing.

As I made my way back on to I-25, I began praying that the Lord would bless him with a good job and save his soul.

Not too long after I left the hitch-hiker, I was suddenly caught up into a mighty vision. God began showing me things that were coming in my future. He gave me visions and revelations of what I would be doing in the future. I was amazed! I could hardly comprehend all that I saw. It was rewarding, beautiful, exciting, thrilling and powerful. I trembled! I was astounded by what God revealed to me. I thought "how could He use **me**?" I was nothing. I still wonder to this day how my car maintained control. I was there, but my mind and heart had been taken captive by God. Perhaps the Lord, or a host of angels (the Lord's secret agents), guided my car.

In the vision, I was an overseer of God's Word. How could this be? I had no degree or schooling in the Word of God. Surely, I was the least qualified of all people. But God was there with me in my car revealing the future. It was real. I was there when it happened so I know what I'm writing is true. I accepted God's plan for me because I had been called of God.

> "He staggered not at the promise of God through unbelief; but was strong in faith, giving glory to God; And being fully persuaded that, what he had promised, he was able also to perform." (Rom. 4:20-21)

My mind went back to that little Southern Baptist Church in Boulder, Colorado—to the night when I had heard the preacher's message, "How Far Would You Go with Jesus

Christ." I agreed with God that night. I accepted the whole Bible, not knowing what He might ask me to do. Yes, I sold out to follow Jesus Christ forever.

I was deeply challenged by his message. I thought about my past as an illiterate and feeling worthless without an education. I was going from job to job without satisfaction or purpose. So I agreed with that preacher's message. I said, "Ok, God, you're on! I'm going to put my trust in you, and I'll do whatever your Word says to do."

I walked out of church that night, full of faith in a mighty God and desiring to be obedient in following His Word. I walked over to my car and was reaching for the car door when the Holy Spirit spoke to me. I didn't know much about the Holy Spirit at the time. He became a powerful resource after reading the Word of God, and I learned to obey the same soft voice many more times as He helped me clean up my sinful life. The Word confirmed the voice I heard. I found in the Book of Revelation that the Lord will chasten those He loves.

> "As many as I love, I rebuke and chasten: be zealous therefore, and repent. Behold, I stand at the door, and knock: if any man hear my voice, and open the door, I will come in to him, and will sup with him, and he with me." (Rev. 3:19-20)

He said, "If you're going to challenge me, what about those cigarettes in your shirt pocket?" I was amazed that He knew what was underneath my suit jacket. I quickly took the cigarettes out of my shirt pocket and threw them in the gutter next to the car. At my apartment I cleaned house. I threw a new carton of cigarettes and ash trays out in a dumpster for trash removal. It has been over 45 years and I have not touched a cigarette since that night.

At the time, I was working for a company selling a large variety of books and magazines to supermarkets, convenience stores and drugstores. Then it hit me. What will I do about the pornography? In their mix of printed material they also sold skin magazines. I was a route serviceman for the company. How could I, a Christian, remain righteous, pure and holy—and deal with this? I had a big problem.

> "He that believeth on him is not condemned: but he that believeth not is condemned already, because he hath not believed in the name of the only begotten Son of God. And this is the condemnation, that light is come into the world, and men loved darkness rather than light, because their deeds were evil.
>
> "For every one that doeth evil hateth the light, neither cometh to the light, lest his deeds should be reproved. But he that doeth truth cometh to the light, that his deeds may be made manifest, that they are wrought in God." (John 3:18-21)

Well, I knew the company was in darkness, and those skin magazines were the evidence. I wondered how I could oversee God's Word while working with people who loved darkness rather than the light. It didn't fit the picture of holiness in God's Holy Word that I had been reading about in the Book of Romans.

> "I beseech you therefore, brethren, by the mercies of God, that ye present your bodies a living sacrifice, holy, acceptable unto God, which is your reasonable service. And be not conformed to this world: but be ye transformed by the renewing of your mind, that ye may prove what is that good, and acceptable, and perfect, will of God." (Rom. 12:1-2)

My steps were now ordered by the Lord. I had trusted in myself for the previous twenty-six years—now it was time to trust Him. Then the Lord made it known to me that I should not tell anyone about the visions and revelations. So, I just pondered them in my heart and waited on the Lord as I continued to follow the dictates of the Holy Spirit.

Over the next several months, I studied the Word, went to Sunday school and listened to a multitude of sermons; all the while, waiting for the visions and revelations to come to fruition.

As time passed, I matured in the knowledge of the Word and developed in the character of the Lord.

"Let us draw near with a true heart in full assurance of faith, having our hearts sprinkled from an evil conscience, and our bodies washed with pure water. Let us hold fast the profession of our faith without wavering; (for he is faithful that promised;) And let us consider one another to provoke unto love and to good works: Not forsaking the assembling of ourselves together, as the manner of some is; but exhorting one another: and so much the more, as ye see the day approaching." (Heb. 10:22-25)

But the secular company I worked for was angry with me because I was defending the truth, calling for righteousness, for all to live in the spirit and not for the flesh. I was in the spirit of God, living for Christ. They were in the carnal flesh, living in darkness and making money on a person's weakness. In this, I found that the carnal flesh hates the Word of God. Why is it that a company would want an employee to be faithful, reliable, honest and true; but wouldn't want anyone mentioning Jesus Christ as the way, the truth and the life?

The light of Christ in me was exposing this darkness of sin. They wanted total liberty to sell filthy magazines and books. I was a hindrance to their liberal views. I believe the Lord wants believers to stand up for holiness and righteousness: at home, in church, in the workplace, in our local communities, in our schools and in government.

My faith and calling were soon challenged. The company was in the dark regarding spiritual things, and was not aware that God had made the gifts of the Spirit available to me. Here is where I discovered the gifts of the Spirit are not for those living in the flesh. The light was on for me and off for them. They thought I was still an illiterate. A few days after I told them that Jesus Christ was now my Lord, they tried to brainwash me (a big mistake). They were doing it because I was now a predictable risk to the promotion and sale of pornography.

I was directed to a conference room with three of the owners, and one began to interrogate me. The interrogation was mentally exhausting. In the process, remaining unruffled was about all I could muster. This was brutal pressure on my brain. I wondered how this could be happening in free America. But power and money cause some people to plot to control others and do things they later regret.

The owner talked relentlessly and persuasively for almost two hours, using carefully chosen words, many of which seemed to be intellectual and purposely aimed to be way over my head; including speaking of my mom, apple pie and God as objects unworthy of love and trust. He said all this at the end to cause an angry outburst. When he finished he was completely spent, and I was near explosion. The pressure was greater than a human could bear. At this point I was far past the final stage of anger, but had not yet revealed my feelings.

Finally, I was forced to give an answer. I didn't know what to say or do. Thus, in secret prayer, I cried out to Almighty God for help. The Holy Spirit came right above me. I knew He was there! He sent a word to me from above my head. The word the Holy Spirit gave me was, "humble."

I used that word in my answer to the interrogator. I said, "I will humble myself to you, and you can tell me what to do."

The interrogator's face flushed red, and then turned black. He couldn't have anticipated my answer in a million years. He had held nothing back to try to set me to blow off in a rage. He was embarrassed! He was baffled and frustrated that his countless words did not move me. I sat there trusting God. I thought he was going to die. I somehow knew his words to destroy me were over. I went over to him and said I love you. He stood speechless. He didn't know that the Holy Ghost was there to help me. The secret was mine. I quietly left for a weekend of prayer and waited to see what the Lord would take me through next.

> "But when they shall lead you, and deliver you up, take no thought beforehand what ye shall speak, neither do ye premeditate: but whatsoever shall be given you in that hour, that speak ye: for it is not ye that speak, but the Holy Ghost." (Mark 13:11)

I continued to be a faithful employee to that same man for ten more years, but I worked to destroy the works of the flesh while promoting good housekeeping.

Man will complicate things to keep you from finding the truth. He will intimidate you with all his learning and use you for his own gain. Therefore, God sometimes takes issue when those who are the learned take advantage of the unlearned.

The gifts of the Spirit are like secret spiritual agents that drop in when faith is calling. Think about it! I had no education in business. The gifts of the Spirit came as real-time data from God when faith called help! "I can do all things through Christ which strengtheneth me." (Phil. 4:13)

The secret the interrogator didn't know was that just days before the meeting, I had been **called of God**. I was waiting on the Lord for what He had promised me. I had secret knowledge and wisdom through the call of God. The call from God made me privy to something that was going to happen in my life. I foreknew what it was and no one else did! It was top secret. I didn't tell a living soul.

Moreover, the promise had not yet come to pass; so all I could do was wait on God, and not be moved by the words or actions of man, or what they would say or do to me that did not fit the conditions of the divine promise of God. I was safe, secure and at rest; I knew God would protect me. I knew the promise would eventually come to pass. It was equally difficult to remain patient in the wait; but joy and peace came to me when I saw my secret had confounded the carnal conceited wisdom of man.

> "Thou shalt hide them in the secret of thy presence from the pride of man: thou shalt keep them secretly in a pavilion from the strife of tongues." (Ps. 31:20)
>
> "The secret of the LORD is with them that fear him; and he will shew them his covenant." (Ps. 25:14)

The day God came to rescue me has never left my mind. He humbled the enemy right before my eyes. It was amazing to see. My employer thought I could read his mind or had read his mail. The Holy Spirit knew his plan and what he was thinking. He was there for me when I needed spiritual help. One of the owners that witnessed this meeting trembled as I walked past him the following week. The majority owner smiled when he first saw me a few days after that earth shaking meeting.

I believe God is always watching to protect His children if the enemy tries to do them harm. Israel has an amazing history of God defending His people time and time again. He still does so today. When will the enemy learn not to interfere with a servant of the Lord?

I'm so glad I'm on the Lord's side. The Lord gave me a Bible lesson that day that remains real to this day. When he gave me the word humble, I discovered in a single day that God is Omniscient, Omnipotent and Omnipresent. The word humble was the perfect response. It was powerful. He is there when we need Him. He is faithful and trustworthy. All glory, praise and honor to Jesus Christ.

When Paul was bitten by that snake, shook the beast off into the fire and acted as though nothing had happened, he astounded those around him. They thought he would die.

But we see the angel of God had given him a prophetic word of wisdom the night before, that he would testify in Rome about the Lord Jesus Christ. Therefore, he foreknew that no harm would come to him. He knew he could not die, at least until after speaking in Rome.

It is a comfort to know that God knows our future. We don't have to live in fear of this world's economy. We can live in God's economy. When we put our faith and trust in God, we have His protection and care.

From that terrible day of interrogation, I found the Holy Spirit to be my personal attorney and counselor. He was there to speak on my behalf and gave me a word of wisdom—humble. It gave me wisdom and knowledge of the kingdom of God, which is righteousness and peace and joy in the Holy Ghost.

> "Howbeit when he, the Spirit of truth, is come, he will guide you into all truth: for he shall not speak of himself; but whatsoever he shall hear, that shall he

speak: and he will shew you things to come." (John 16:13)

It is so good to know that what God tells a believer to do is not common knowledge to the enemy. The enemy has no power to enter our brain, twist things around and confuse the call.

He will show you things to come; this is a word of wisdom (future). This is why we should spend precious time in prayer, being obedient to the dictates of the Holy Spirit. Then we will have a sure foundation of walking in the Word. He will keep our heart at peace, having joy with discoveries of the knowledge and wisdom of God.

The man who interrogated me served an inferior commander (old Satan). In the ensuing days, he and his family were awakened in the early morning hours by their barking dog. Their lives were spared as their house burned to the ground. Then a few days later, he got boils all over his body. His suffering was visible. I could clearly see he was lost and without the knowledge of the things of God.

God gave me a special love and forgiveness toward this man. I've prayed many times for the salvation of his soul. I know that God forgives. If not for the saving power of Christ, where would I be?

My interrogator had yielded to temptation and was subject to the enticement of the enemy. The devil had led him astray. He was deceived. He may have secretly planned to take full control of the company from the other owners. The love of money may have caused him to do this evil that brought about his great fall.

> <u>"For the love of money is the root of all evil: which while some coveted after, they have erred from the faith, and pierced themselves through with many sorrows." (1 Tim. 6:10)</u>

Many years later, God moved me from that company and had me start a Christian book and Bible distribution company. I continued to pray and witness to this man for many years. I even sent him some of my Country Gospel tapes that I recorded in Nashville. My prayer is that he answered the call from our blessed Redeemer.

THE ABSOLUTES

1. **The call** of God called Paul to be seen and heard as an apostle of Jesus Christ.
2. **The call** kept the message of the cross as the object of faith.
3. **The call** represented the Holy Word of God.
4. **The call** is Christ in me and me in Christ.
5. **The call** of the Word is the only thing that can prick the flesh.
6. **The call** kept Paul walking in the Spirit.
7. **The call** caused Paul to live faithfully, in the Spirit, in Christ and not in the flesh.
8. **The call** came to Paul to write the Word of God.
9. **The call** showed Paul how to live as the Gospel, requires pure and holy.
10. **The call** reminded Paul to obey the spirit of truth, the vision and revelation of God.
11. **The call** has a boundary to keep conversations sanctified.

12. **The call** knows the boundary of the measure of the call of God.
13. **The call** is the Gospel with a boundary fenced in with love.
14. **The call** is for God's purpose only.
15. **The call** kept Satan out of the game plan, fleeing because he was resisted.
16. **The call** defeated Satan.
17. **The call** kept Paul out of fleshly living.
18. **The call** came against all reasons the flesh could give for not obeying **the call.**
19. **The call** will always be working to have the Spirit-man in authority and in control, not the flesh-man.
20. **The call** has dominion over the sin nature.
21. **The call** reminds man his character must be as the Word.
22. God watches over the Word to perform **the call.**
23. **The call** makes the will of man supple and willing to serve God.
24. **The call** kept Paul pressing towards the mark for the prize of the high calling of God in Christ Jesus.
25. **The call** is to live in the rose above the thorn.

JESUS IS THE ROSE ABOVE THE THORN

"For the vision is yet for an appointed time, but at the end it shall speak, and not lie: though it tarry, wait for it; because it will surely come, it will not tarry." (Hab. 2:3)

Jesus Christ is the rose above the thorn. The call is the first part of the thorn. When we are born again by the conviction of the Holy Spirit, we start setting up good housekeeping in the rose; and when we have thoughts and imaginations that conflict with the Word of God, the call of the Holy Spirit and His Word pricks our sin nature (flesh) to get back into the rose; the rose above the thorn.

"I am the rose of Sharon, and the lily of the valleys. As the lily among thorns, so is my love among the daughters. As the apple tree among the trees of the

> wood, so is my beloved among the sons. I sat down under his shadow with great delight, and his fruit was sweet to my taste. He brought me to the banqueting house, and his banner over me was love." (Song 2:1-4)

To our sons and daughters He is the rose of Sharon, and the lily of the valley. He is our redeemer. He helps us ride out the storms of life and is a true friend, a daily companion to walk with in love, reaching out to others. He is the rose above the thorn.

By living in the Spirit of the Living God, a firewall of the Blood of Christ—the cross, the death and the resurrected Christ—surrounds us so Satan cannot pass or do harm. Our first—born sin nature is locked out by the declaration of the cross and the law of the Spirit of life in Christ. He is forever with us as we live in the rose above the thorn.

We must never forget the Words of the Lord or His works. The only time we should look back at the past is to consider all that God has done for us. In Christ we have everything to succeed. We should believe God for greater works than these. It would be an insult to God not to show our love and dedication to His word and work.

When Moses led the children of Israel out of Egypt, they soon forgot the works of the Lord. If we live to please God instead of the flesh, it will protect us from having leanness in our soul.

> "Then believed they his words; they sang his praise. They soon forgat his works; they waited not for his counsel: But lusted exceedingly in the wilderness, and tempted God in the desert. And he gave them their request; but sent leanness into their soul." (Ps. 106:12-15)
>
> "Submit yourselves therefore to God. Resist the devil, and he will flee from you. Draw nigh to God, and he will draw nigh to you. Cleanse your hands, ye sinners; and purify your hearts, ye double minded.
>
> "Be afflicted, and mourn, and weep: let your laughter be turned to mourning, and your joy to heaviness. Humble yourselves in the sight of the Lord, and he shall lift you up." (James 4:7-10)

The perfect man is one who is serious and sincere in baptism. In baptism you bury the old man, the old nature and all of your past sin. You come up out of the water a new creature in Christ. Old things are passed away, and behold, all things have become new. The law of the Spirit of life in Christ gives us dominion over our old sin nature.

It is like going to your own funeral every day. You see yourself dead to the things that used to exalt the flesh. Those things don't move you anymore. You're dead to them! Then every day you walk where only the Word lives and the rose of Sharon blooms.

The problem some never come to understand is that they often go back to some of the same old sin-laden places where the flesh is tempted and resurrected once again. If that occurs, you crucify the Lord Jesus Christ all over again.

> <u>"Therefore leaving the principles of the doctrine of Christ, let us go on unto perfection; not laying again the foundation of repentance from dead works, and of faith toward God," (Heb. 6:1)</u>

Remembering that we have purpose in Christ and a mission to fulfill, is what keeps us focused. When some evil force that is contrary to the call of God is trying to persuade us to disobey God's will, the cross is our victory, and the Holy Spirit will be there to guide us through it.

I got an amazing victory when the secular company was attempting to brainwash me. The sales manager caused me to boil inside like a volcano burning with anger; but instead of exploding by way of the sin nature, I prayed to God in the spirit. The answer "humble" came by way of the Holy Spirit as a word of wisdom and not by an infirmity, poor eyesight, some physical weakness of the flesh or Satan inciting a person to inflict pain to make me eat crow to stay humble.

"Wherefore I also, after I heard of your faith in the Lord Jesus, and love unto all the saints, Cease not to give thanks for you, making mention of you in my prayers; That the God of our Lord Jesus Christ, the Father of glory, may give unto you the spirit of wisdom and revelation in the knowledge of him:" (Eph. 1:15-17)

PRAYER

Our righteous heavenly Father,
We give glory and honor to your name. You are worthy of our praise. You are Holy. It is you we worship. It is you who saves to the uttermost. We thank you for the forgiveness of sin and for cleansing us of all unrighteousness. We forsake our former ways and now seek to follow the example of Christ and your Holy Word.

We abide in Christ—the rose of Sharon, the lily of the valley; the rose above the thorn. Your Word is engraved upon our hearts. Our thoughts are on what is true and honest, just, pure and lovely. We find joy in the Holy Ghost—in the praises and testimonies of your work, power and mighty hand. Our thoughts are on you, the cross and things above. We sing hymns and spiritual songs of our redeemer and rejoice while we wait for the coming of our Lord.

We pray for our character to be supple and molded by being obedient to the Word. Lord, help us to keep ourselves pure and unspotted from the things of this world. Open our understanding as we read and meditate day and night upon your Holy Word. Lord, direct our steps to please you in all that we say and do.

We pray for our family tree: for our children and grandchildren to know you, and to walk with you like Enoch did in pleasing you. We pray for our friends and neighbors to be found in your righteousness, peace and joy; that our nation would humble itself and forsake all wickedness and evil, and repent of sin.

Lord, as your ambassadors, we visit the fatherless and widows in their affliction and pray for their safety and care. We remember and give to the poor. We are burdened for the lost and pray that they will be drawn to you through your Word.

Now, hold our hand, dear Lord, when the way is dark all around us; for as we step into the unknown, we trust and believe in faith that at that moment your light will shine upon our path that lets us know you direct our paths to lead the way. Strengthen us when the load is too heavy.

In Jesus' name we pray, Amen.

SOURCE NOTES

THE KING JAMES HOLY BIBLE

Hedonism: Merriam-Webster's 11th Collegiate Dictionary.
Humility: Merriam-Webster's 11th Collegiate Dictionary.
Egotism: Merriam-Webster's 11th Collegiate Dictionary.
Infirmity: Merriam-Webster's 11th Collegiate Dictionary.
My Utmost for His Highest - Oswald Chambers.
Supple: Merriam-Webster's 11th Collegiate Dictionary.

LaVergne, TN USA
13 December 2009

166833LV00001B/2/P